THE PROFESSIONAL TRAVEL ADVISOR GUIDEBOOK

Learn About Industry Insights, Operations, and How To Become a Professional Travel Advisor

TAYLOR BECKETT

FOUNDER OF LUXURY CORPORATE TRAVEL

A KIHEI PRESS BOOK

Publishing Page

ISBN	Paperback	979-8-9907317-0-7
IBSN	Hardcover	979-8-9907317-1-4
ISBN	E-book	979-8-9907317-2-1
ISBN	Audiobook	979-8-9907317-3-8

Library of Congress Control Number: 2024912090

First Edition
Printed in the United States of America

Kihei Press books can be purchased at discounted rates for large orders. Signed copies and special editions can also be ordered upon request. For more information, contact Kihei Press at kiheipress.com.

Dedication

This book is dedicated to:

My Dad, for instilling an unbreakable work ethic in me.

My Mom, for giving me the right perspective and value of time in life.

My Sister, for giving me the desire to live without excess.

My Wife, for her support, knowledge, and love.

Contents

WHO IS THIS BOOK FOR?

This book is for individuals who are interested in entering the travel industry and becoming a professional travel advisor.

Though you do not need to be well traveled to become a professional travel advisor, most enter the field after extensive personal travel. You may also have experienced your friends and family continuously saying that you would be great at this type of work after helping plan their vacations. Similarly, after helping so many people plan their travel, you may come to realize that this occupation is something you could both enjoy and excel at.

Additionally, if any of the following statements interest you, this is the book for you.

- You want to learn about the various types of professional opportunities that exist for travel advisors.

- You want to know where to begin and what the requirements are to become a travel advisor.

- You are curious about all of the tools and resources available to travel advisors that are not accessible to the general public.

While this book is mainly for those just getting started, this book can even be of benefit to current travel advisors. For those advisors looking for continuing education and professional development, hopefully you can learn something new and advance your expertise in the industry by reading the following content in this book.

Foreword

Welcome fellow travelers, adventure seekers, wanderers, and professional vacationers! If you've purchased this book, you're probably considering becoming a travel advisor. Congratulations! You've picked the perfect place to start.

In a world inundated with online resources like Google, social media, and TripAdvisor, you might be wondering, "Who even uses travel advisors anymore?" The answer to that question is: people who understand the value travel advisors provide. Why not just ask someone who already knows the answers? Why spend hours researching new destinations and risk making a poor choice when an advisor can provide you with the best recommendations? Why spend more money when you could save instead?

This is where you step in with all the knowledge you will gain from this book and plan a trip that will knock their socks off. Taylor Beckett is undoubtedly one of the greatest resources one can utilize when beginning this journey. You've got questions, he's got answers, and he's written them all down in one convenient location.

When I met Taylor, I had been considering becoming a travel advisor and decided to contact him about signing on with his agency. Immediately after our first conversation, I was hooked. We talked about some of our favorite places and what we loved about traveling. He answered what I like to call the "first round" of my incessant questions, and shared so much insight that helped put my mind at ease.

I can honestly say with absolute certainty that I couldn't have done it without Taylor and all of his advice, tips, and guidance. I wish I would've had this book to reference when I first started, but thankfully, it is now available to you to answer all of your questions about the travel advising industry.

There are few things that I love more in life than sunshine and exploring a new place. I have been to 18 countries thus far and have seen and experienced some of the most breathtakingly gorgeous places you could ever imagine. I've experienced countless stunning sunsets and swam in waterfalls all across the globe. I've had a monkey try to steal food out of my bag in Thailand and been in Italy for a week with no luggage. You name it, I've seen it.

Not only did these experiences give me a good anecdote, but they also taught me so many lessons along the way. Sharing the story of "The Great Mexico Mishap of 2014," where a misplaced customs paper resulted in one of the most chaotic travel days of my life and a missed connecting flight (not to mention a near divorce when my husband realized what I'd done), paints a very clear picture of the importance of documentation in a foreign country - one that is not soon forgotten. Sometimes the lesson is as simple as remembering to pack a change of clothes and all your essentials in a carry-on. Sometimes the lesson is that just because the flight is cheap, doesn't mean that you should take it.

Each of these experiences and lessons have equipped me with knowledge and resources to provide value to my clients and book those once-in-a-lifetime trips.

These experiences, and the knowledge I've gained from working with Taylor, have proven to be the key to my success.

I am forever grateful for the opportunity to learn from him and believe that this will be what sets me apart from every other travel advisor. It can be a daunting and overwhelming task to find somewhere to start, but with this book guiding you, you're sure to set yourself up for success.

If you passionately believe that no amount of money could ever replace the memories made while traveling, and that being off the beaten path leads to some of the greatest adventures, then I suggest you keep reading. As an experienced traveler, one of the greatest opportunities you have is to share what you know with others.

Sincerely,
Brittany Morrison

Introduction

Born into a family of aviation, travel has been a part of my life since the day life began for me. Now, thirty years later, I am still seeking out the unique experiences, cultures, and perspectives that traveling provides.

One of the questions I get asked most often nowadays is where the best place I've traveled to is. If I had to give just one answer, it would be Australia. With a passion for wildlife and animal encounters, there are only a handful of other countries that can compete with the animal experiences that Australia has to offer. As an added bonus, the food is first-class and the country is surrounded by coastline and pristine beaches.

Pictured Above: Taylor Beckett and Esther Beckett (wife) at the Lone Pine Koala Sanctuary in Brisbane, Australia (2022).

Though I believe Australia wins my overall top spot, South Africa should not be left out of the conversation, especially with the wildlife and safari offerings that are at the top of so many people's bucket list.

Pictured on the right: Taylor Beckett with an adult male cheetah at a wildlife conservation area just east of Cape Town, South Africa (2023).

As a professional travel advisor, I love being asked what my favorite locations and things to do are. These places and experiences normally hold some of my best life memories. Being able to be continually reminded of those moments and who I share them with, really keeps my life at peace.

People close to me know me as a man of extremely few words. I believe it is in part due to wanting to be completely aware of my surroundings and to minimize my distractions. I believe the other part is wanting to take in the views, experiences, and values of others, which I suspect originates from how I operate when traveling.

Though my words are few in person, I enjoyed all the time it took to put this book's worth of words together on paper.

The story behind writing *The Professional Travel Advisor Guidebook* came to life a few years after I officially founded my U.S. based travel company, Luxury

Corporate Travel. After meeting countless people who had the desire to become travel advisors, and allowing my agency to host advisors, I realized how valuable a guidebook would be.

Hearing everyone's questions reminded me of the beginning of my travel advisor days and the thousands of unanswered questions I was seeking answers to back then.

Before I became a travel advisor, I was working in the travel industry as an airline pilot. Though I had been to somewhere around 50 countries and felt like I knew every flight, hotel, and popular spot that existed, I still had no idea what I needed to do to become a professional travel advisor.

Looking back on it now, I wish I would have had this guidebook to help me navigate where I am today. Without it, I found myself doing web search after web search, trying to piece together all of the information I was looking for.

During my initial search, I was shocked to find out that independent travel advisors could provide their professional services free of charge to travelers, while still being paid by travel suppliers. That moment sent my mind into overdrive, thinking about all of the potential opportunities and value that could be created.

For the most part, people will benefit when using a professional industry expert for a life task, when compared to doing that task themselves. For example: a professional chef can most likely make a better tasting dinner than you can, a doctor can perform surgery better than you can, and a professional pilot can fly you across the country better than you can.

Because those professionals provide enough value to do a task much better than we can, we are willing to pay a pretty penny for their services. As travel advisors, not only do we have that exact same opportunity to provide value as a travel professional, we are also able to offer our services free of charge. This allows us to create even more value to our travelers, as our expertise and services come at absolutely no charge to them.

That being said, some travel advisors do charge a fee for their services, even though they are already being paid by suppliers. This is 100% acceptable, as more likely than not, the value they are providing for their services outweighs the cost. That is why people are willing to pay for them.

Like in any field, there will be people towards the top end of the performance scale and others towards the bottom end of the scale. If you had to choose between a travel advisor who didn't charge a fee but didn't provide any value to you, or another advisor that charged a fee but saved you 30% on your booking, moved you from a three-star to a five-star hotel, and had a bottle of Champagne waiting for you in your room, you probably would pick the higher performing and, most likely, more experienced advisor.

Though most of my time today is spent running the day to day operations of my company, I keep to my mission of getting the best value for the travelers I still advise for. My goal is to always be at the top of that performance scale.

It is important to remember how big of a difference you can make in people's lives in this profession. Normally, people will travel with those closest to them during their time away from work to rest, recover, explore, and decompress together. These periods of time are usually a person's most valued moments each year, thus the significant impact that can be made by you.

I know there are others out there that understand this purpose and seek the value that this profession provides to both yourself and others.

This book is structured to allow the readers to make up their own mind about the general information that is presented to them. I will insert my personal opinion from time to time, but my overall goal is to be able to effectively pass on all of the information I have learned about this profession over the years into a readable (hopefully enjoyable) 200 page book.

Though some readers may be well-versed in the content provided throughout, I hope you can take away at least one thing in the following pages that will enhance either you or your travelers' future quality of life.

So for those of you who are interested in entering the travel industry and learning how to become a professional travel advisor, here is my book to you!

-Taylor Beckett

P.S.

- Yes, the discounts are awesome.
- Yes, you can work from home, or anywhere in the world really.
- Yes, you can make really good money.

1

Like many other professional career fields that require a type of license or certification to legally operate in their respective fields, travel advising is no different. Thankfully, for those interested in the travel trade industry, certification and accreditation are very easy to obtain when compared to other fields that require years of schooling, on the job shadowing, or a series of rigorous tests, prior to beginning work.

The big three questions many potential advisors initially search for are the following:

1. Do I need to have a license or obtain credentials?

2. Do I need to go to school or graduate from a travel advisor training program?

3. Do I need to have any sort of experience or previous qualification?

One of the problems you may run into in your initial search for these answers is that each question could be answered by either yes or no, as it varies from person to person. The biggest factor being your decision to either work for yourself, or choosing to work for someone else.

If you have already begun your search for the questions above, then more likely than not, the first thing you've probably seen pop up on your results page are the travel advisor industry accreditation agencies.

In the United States, there are four main travel advisor and travel agency accreditation organizations.

- International Air Transport Association (IATA)

- Cruise Lines International Association (CLIA)

- Airlines Reporting Corporation (ARC)

- Computerized Corporate Rate Association (CCRA)

Of these four main accreditation organizations, each issues a variety of different credentials. The two main types of credentials they each issue are: an agency accreditation and an individual agent accreditation.

For aspiring travel advisors, one of the first decisions you have to make is to determine the type of credential you would like to obtain (if one is needed) and identify the eligibility requirements for your chosen credential.

To help you pinpoint which credential is the right match and to know what you are eligible for, the first question you need to answer is this:

Do you want to start your own agency or do you want to work for an established agency or travel supplier?

This question can be hard to answer, especially at the beginning of your journey, when you are unaware of all of the industry opportunities. The following are seven of the most common paths for travel advisors:

1. Working for an established travel agency as an employee.

2. Working for an established host agency as an independent contractor.

3. Working as an employee for an established travel industry supplier (example: hotel, cruise line, airline, train operator, tour company).

4. Working as an employee for an established travel industry vendor (example: wholesalers and vacation package companies).

5. Working as an employee for a non-travel industry corporation, managing company-specific travel.

6. Starting your own agency.

7. Purchasing a franchise.

For the most part, these seven paths can be divided into two separate categories in regards to accreditation. Typically, if you are employed by someone else, accreditation is either taken care of by the employer or is not required.

Professional travel advisors wishing to work as independent advisors with a host agency, purchasing a franchise, or starting their own agency, will likely need some form of accreditation.

If you are still unsure of which path to take, the remaining chapters in this book will explain and compare the options above to help you decide the course you would like to pursue.

Currently, the most popular option for first time leisure travel advisors is to join an established host agency. Host agencies are accredited travel agencies that allow individual travel advisors access to the host agency accreditation number for bookings.

This option is attractive to many, as it offers the individual travel advisor one of the quickest ways to begin booking travel. Additionally, host agencies can provide a variety of benefits that are extremely helpful to first time advisors:

- **Higher Commission Rates** - Travel suppliers normally offer commission tiers based on agency productivity. This means that the more bookings that are registered by the agency for a particular supplier, the higher the commission rate for advisors making bookings with the same supplier using the host agency accreditation number.

- **Lower Startup Cost** - Due to not having to pay for agency accreditation, seller of travel licenses and other agency expenses.

- **Access To Travel Consortium Benefits** - If the host agency pays for a travel consortium membership, consortium benefits are available to all of the contracted individual travel advisors.

- **Assistance & Support** - In my opinion, this is the most valuable benefit. The industry experience of the host agency allows it to help answer any questions you have and offer support when you need it.

When seeking your individual advisor credentials through a host agency, the host will be the one to approve your application after submission to the accreditation agency.

Before choosing a host agency and requesting your individual credentials, be sure to ask what consortium the host is a member of, as these are very valuable associations to be a part of.

In short: travel consortia are organizations that use the collective booking power of individual agencies to negotiate higher commission rates from suppliers, preferred client benefits (value adds), and provide a wealth of resources and training to individual advisors. Select consortia will even offer dedicated booking portals, in lieu of booking directly with a supplier.

Below are a few of the key benefits consortia provide to both agencies and advisors:

Consortium Rate Codes & Client Perks

One of the most popular features consortia provide are complementary client perks and value-added hotel rate codes. These negotiated hotel rate codes normally include the following:

- Amenity or Property Credit, Typically $100
- Welcome Gift or Amenity

- Complimentary Breakfast
- Upgrade (If Available)
- Early Check-In and Late Check-Out
- Complimentary Wi-Fi

One of the great aspects of the consortium rate codes is that they normally populate the exact same rate as the hotel's public standard nightly rate. This means that if the hotel has the regular member rate for one night set at $290, you are able to add in all of the benefits listed above for the same nightly rate of $290. These rate codes are booked directly with the hotel which ensures your clients will also receive their loyalty points and status accruals.

Consortia will also negotiate complimentary perks for cruises and tour companies. They usually include the following:

- On-board Credits
- Prepaid Gratuities
- Bonus Amenities and Welcome Gifts

Training

Consortia provide both in-person and online training on a variety of topics and travel specialties. These courses help educate the advisor on both the consortia tools and resources, as well as industry topics and advisor operations. Additionally, consortia will negotiate discounts and complementary training courses offered by accreditation agencies.

Resources

One the best resources consortia provide is the direct contact details to supplier trade support staff. These are the people you contact when you need help or information from a specific supplier that you are booking with. (Their information is normally difficult to locate otherwise).

Higher Base Commission Rates

Normally, agencies are given the same base commission rate with a supplier, unless they send enough business to the supplier to qualify for a higher commission tier. Consortia are able to negotiate higher commission base tiers so that the agency can earn higher levels of commission, before entering higher tiers.

Booking Portals

Specifically when looking at boutique and non-chain hotels that do not provide the ability to attach agency accreditation numbers online, having a commissionable booking portal available through a consortium is a fantastic asset to have access to.

Client Leads & Online Profiles

If you are looking to network with clients outside of your current connections, consortia provide online agent listing tools that allow potential clients the ability to locate you based on your location, travel experience, certifications, and specialties.

Marketing

Whether you are trying to market to current clients or potential clients, consortia provide a variety of different methods to market to travelers. Marketing options normally include: direct mail (magazines, brochures, postcards), email, and social media assets.

Industry Discounts & FAM Opportunities

If you elect to utilize Customer Relationship Management (CRM) software to manage client information, itineraries, and payments, consortia normally will provide discounted access to the most popular programs. Suppliers will also collaborate with consortia to offer supplier familiarization trips (FAMs) to advisors looking to increase their product knowledge and experience to help send more clients to those suppliers.

In addition to consortia, there are other professional industry organizations you can elect to join that provide valuable benefits to both agencies and individual travel advisors. Below are a just few examples of benefits that may be available through a professional organization:

- Insurance (Business/Professional, Health, Life, Accident, Long Term Care)

- Resources (Legal, Operational)

- Training & Education (Online and In-Person Courses)

- Growth Tools (Conference and Networking Events, Online Advisor Listings, and Industry Credibility)

- Career Opportunities (Both within the organization and through member job boards)

- Discounts (General business products as well as industry and occupational specific tools)

Below is a list of popular industry associations based both domestically and internationally.

Domestic Organizations

- Adventure Travel Trade Association (ATTA)
- Airlines Reporting Corporation (ARC)
- Alaska Travel Industry Association (ATIA)
- American Society of Travel Advisors (ASTA)
- Arizona Lodging and Tourism Association (AzLTA)
- California Travel Association (CTA)
- Computerized Corporate Rate Association (CCRA)
- Cruise Lines International Association (CLIA)
- Family Travel Association (FTA)
- Global Business Travel Association (GBTA)
- Hawaii Lodging & Tourism Association (HLTA)
- Indiana Tourism Association (ITA)
- International Air Transport Association (IATA)
- Kentucky Travel Industry Association (KTIA)
- Louisiana Travel Association (LTA)
- Maine Tourism Association (MTA)

- Maryland Tourism Coalition (MTC)
- Medical Tourism Association (MTA)
- Mississippi Tourism Association (MTA)
- National Tour Association (NTA)
- Nebraska Travel Association (NETA)
- North Carolina Travel Industry Association (NCTIA)
- Ohio Travel Association (OTA)
- Oklahoma Travel Industry Association (OTIA)
- Oregon Tour and Travel Alliance (OTTA)
- Sports Events & Tourism Association (Sports ETA)
- Student & Youth Travel Association (SYTA)
- Tennessee Hospitality & Tourism Association (TNHTA)
- Texas Travel Alliance (TTA)
- Travel & Tourism Research Association (TTRA)
- Travel Industry Association of Florida
- Utah Tourism Industry Association (UTIA)
- U.S. Travel Association
- Wellness Tourism Association (WTA)
- West Virginia Hospitality & Travel Association (WVHTA)

International Organizations

- Albanian Tour Operator Association (ATOA)
- Association of Bahrain Tour and Travel Agents (ABTTA)
- Association of Belgian Tour Operators (ABTO)
- Association of Bhutanese Tour Operators (ABTO)
- Association of Brazilian Travel Agents (ABAV)
- Association of British Travel Agents (ABTA)
- Association of Bulgarian Tour Operators (ABTTA)

- Association of Canadian Travel Agencies (ACTA)
- Association of Croatian Travel Agencies (UHPA)
- Association of Cyprus Travel Agents (ACTA)
- Association of Czech Travel Agents (ACK)
- Association of Danish Travel Agents (DRF)
- Association of Finnish Travel Industry (SMAL)
- Association of Hungarian Travel Agencies (MUISZ)
- Association of Latvian Travel Agents (ALTA)
- Association of Namibian Travel Agents (ANTA)
- Association of Slovenian Travel Agencies (ZTAS)
- Association of South African Travel Agents (ASATA)
- Association of Swedish Travel Agents (SRF)
- Association of Travel Companies of Moldova (ANAT)
- Association of Travel Agencies of Andorra (AAVA)
- Association of Travel Agencies of Azerbaijan (ATAA)
- Association of Travel Agents of Bangladesh (ATAB)
- Association of Travel Agencies of Ecuador (ASECUT)
- Association of Turkish Travel Agents (TURSAB)
- Association of Zimbabwe Travel Agents (AZTA)
- Australian Travel Industry Association (ATIA)
- China Association of Travel Services (CATS)
- Colombian Association of Travel Agencies (ANATO)
- Costa Rican Association of Travel Agencies (ACAV)
- Dubai Travel and Tour Agents Group (DTTAG)
- Dutch Association of Travel Agents (ANVR)
- Egyptian Travel Agents Association (ETTA)
- Estonian Travel and Tourism Association (ETFL)
- Ethiopian Travel Agents Association (ETAA)

- German Travel Association (DRV)
- Ghana Association of Travel Agents (GATTA)
- Hellenic Association of Travel Agencies (HATTA)
- Icelandic Travel Industry Association (SAF)
- Iran Tour Operators Association (ITOA)
- Irish Travel Agents Association (ITAA)
- Israel Association of Travel Agencies (ITTAA)
- Japan Association of Travel Agents (JATA)
- Jordan Society of Tourism and Travel Agents (JSTA)
- Kenya Association of Travel Agents (KATA)
- Korea Association of Travel Agents (KATA)
- Kyrgyz Association of Tour Operators (KATO)
- Lao Association of Travel Agents (LATA)
- Latin American Travel Association (LATA)
- National Association Nigeria Travel Agencies (NANTA)
- National Association Travel Agents Singapore (NATAS)
- Nepal Association of Tour and Travel Agents (NATTA)
- Pacific Asia Travel Association (PATA)
- Peruvian Association of Travel Agencies (APAVIT)
- Philippine Travel Agencies Association (PTAA)
- Portuguese Association of Travel Agencies (APAVT)
- Rwanda Association of Travel Agencies (RATA)
- Serbia National Association of Travel Agencies (YUTA)
- Slovak Association of Travel Agents (SACKA)
- Somalia Association of Travel Tourism Agents (SATTA)
- Spanish Confederation of Travel Agents (CEAV)
- Swiss Federation of Travel Agents (SRV)
- Tanzania Association of Travel Agents (TASOTA)

- Thai Travel Agents Association (TTAA)
- Travel Agents Association of India (TAAI)
- Travel Agents Association of New Zealand (TAANZ)
- Travel Agents Association of Pakistan (TAAP)
- Travel Agents Association of Sri Lanka (TAASL)
- Travel Agents Association of Zambia (TAAZ)
- Travel And Tourism Agencies Council (ATTAC)
- Tunisian Association of Travel Agents (FTAV)
- Uganda Association of Travel Agents (TUGATA)
- Union of Myanmar Travel Association (UMTA)
- Vietnam Society of Travel Agents (VISTA)

Chapter Summary

There are seven main career paths professional travel advisors can select. The one you choose to pursue will determine if you need industry credentials, licenses, training, or previous industry experience.

The following are brief explanations of the different organizations and professional groups in the travel advising industry:

- Travel Suppliers: Hotels, airlines, cruise lines, train operators, tour operators, and rental car companies.

- Travel Vendors: Travel industry companies that sell single or packaged goods and services provided by travel suppliers, sometimes at wholesale rates.

- Travel Agencies: Accredited agencies with industry-recognized credential numbers that can be utilized to earn commission from suppliers.

- Travel Advisors: Professional individuals that can choose to work for a travel supplier, travel vendor, travel agency (either as an employee or independent contractor), or can start their own agency.

- Accreditation Companies: Organizations that suppliers have recognized as a legitimate industry credential issuer.

- Consortia: Organizations that use the collective booking power of individual agencies to negotiate higher commission rates from suppliers, preferred client benefits (value adds), and provide a wealth of resources and training to agencies and individual advisors.

- Industry Organizations: Elective professional associations that provide resources and benefits to their members to help them operate, grow, and succeed in their field of work.

2

This chapter does not apply to travel advisors who will be employed by a company as an employee. That being said, if you are interested in the process that independent contract advisors and travel agencies go through to formally set up their businesses, feel free to include this chapter in your reading.

Luckily, for those who are based in the United States, the process of properly setting up a small business is relatively simple. If your travel business will be the first business you've ever created, it may seem like a daunting task trying to figure out exactly what needs to be done to make your company official and legal.

The good news is that you can turn the entire process into a simple step by step checklist. This ensures that you complete each task in the correct order, as well as helping to alleviate the risk of leaving out an important item.

The first step in the business formation and licensing process is to create a name for your travel company. Once you have picked out your desired name, make sure to check with your current state's business registry to ensure it is not already being used. This will ensure that you do not make the mistake of filing for a business name that is already in use, and thus ultimately rendering it unusable to you.

Additionally, check to see if your chosen business name is available as a domain name on the web, social media handles, and with your desired email operator. Even if you don't plan on operating a website or creating social media pages, this will help identify if someone else has created the same business name as you that was not listed on your state's registry.

Furthermore, checking to see if your business name is in use outside of your state registry will also spare additional potential headaches down the line. Though each agency and travel advisor is issued a unique credential number, having the same name as another travel company already in use may cause unwanted issues with travel suppliers, accreditation organizations, and commission processing partners.

After verifying that your desired company name is available, the next decision you have to make is the type of business structure you would like to create for your travel company. Below are four different types of general business structures in the United States:

- Sole Proprietorship
- Limited Liability Company (LLC)
- Partnership
- Corporation

It may not seem like it at first glance, but your decision regarding the four business structures above will be one of the most important decisions you make for your travel company. Business structures will affect a variety of significant operational factors.

Below are a few general examples of factors that will be affected by your business structure decision:

- Filing Requirements
- Ownership Rules
- Transferability of Ownership Interest
- Formality of Operation
- Taxes
- Liability
- Legal Protection
- Ability to Borrow Money
- Management
- Day-to-Day Operations

Because of the significant impact of these factors, and the fact that different rules apply to different states, the best thing to do before making a decision on your own is to consult both a business attorney and an accountant who specializes in business structures, so that they can provide tailored professional advice that fits your exact needs.

The following descriptions for each type of business structure are general in nature. They are included to help you have a generic understanding of each, so that you can better discuss your needs with a professional. These descriptions should not be treated as a substitute to seeking professional advice.

Sole Proprietorship

A sole proprietorship is the most common form of small business structure in the United States. For the most part, this is due to the fact that business owners are automatically classified as sole proprietors by default, unless they file for another type of business structure.

This means that you are able to operate your travel company as a sole proprietorship without any formal organization. That being said, if you would like to create a trade name for your business, you will be required to file for a Doing Business As (DBA) certificate, with either your county and/or state.

It is important to note that this type of business structure does not produce a separate entity. This is one of the most significant features of a sole proprietorship. Your business assets and liabilities will not be separated from your personal assets and liabilities. As a sole proprietor, you can be held personally liable for your business's liabilities.

Though it is common to see individual travel advisors operating as sole proprietors, it is less common to see travel agencies operating as sole proprietorships. Agencies are more likely to register their company as a Limited Liability Company or LLC.

Limited Liability Company (LLC)

Limited Liability Companies, commonly referred to as LLCs, are business structures that are formed by filling a certificate of formation with the state.

LLCs are the second most popular option for small business owners, after sole proprietorship. The main draw for business owners to file for a LLC is its ability to help protect your personal assets by removing your personal liability from your business operations.

This means that if your travel company ever faced bankruptcy or lawsuits, your personal assets would not be at risk. However, it is important to note that LLCs are business structures that require upkeep and continuous compliance in order to remain valid. If you file for a LLC and neglect the state requirements, or conduct business in a manner that would invalidate the LLC, you open the door to losing your personal liability protection.

Some states will also limit the lifespan of a LLC. This is another distinctive difference from a sole proprietorship. With sole proprietorships, your business structure would continue as long as your business is still operating. With LLCs, that is not always the case.

On your state's LLC formation paperwork, you will notice that the owners of LLCs are identified as members. If a member ever leaves or joins a LLC, select states require the LLC to be dissolved or reformed with the new members. This scenario can occur if you decide to include your spouse, children, or other business partner into the ownership of your company after initial filing, or when you decide to sell or transfer ownership of the LLC.

Though most travel advisors will elect to file for a single member LLC, meaning they are the sole member of the business structure, multiple members can be listed. Additionally, you can elect for your LLC to be member-managed or manager-managed. This choice designates who is in charge of the LLC.

Members of a LLC can be any of the following:

- An Individual
- Trust
- Partnership
- Corporation
- Any Other Commercial or Legal Entity

Most states will default to a member-managed LLC designation, unless you specify otherwise. This means that the members/owners listed in the filling are the managers of the LLC and the ones in charge of all of the decision making.

Managers of an LLC can be any of the following:

- Members/Owners of the LLC
- Third Party Individuals

Though it is extremely uncommon for small travel companies to elect manager-managed LLCs, this designation is available when certain members/owners of the LLC are not participating in the decision making process. This typically occurs when additional family members, who are not running or a part of the business operational decisions, are listed as members/owners of the LLC.

Another notable aspect of LLCs that potentially differ from sole proprietorships is the tax treatment of the business structure. The IRS will treat a LLC, in regards to tax, in one of three ways: either as a partnership, a corporation, or as part of the LLC owner's tax return as a disregarded entity.

By default, there will be no difference in tax treatment between a sole proprietorship and a LLC, for most travel advisors and their travel companies.

If the travel advisor is the only member in the LLC, the IRS will automatically treat the LLC as a disregarded entity. This means that the LLC will be a part of the owner's tax returns, exactly like a sole proprietorship would be. If the advisor would like the LLC to have a different tax classification, he or she can file to change from the default status.

Partnerships

Partnerships are created when two or more people operate a single business together. Normally, partnerships are operated with a partnership agreement between all of the partners. However, there is no requirement for the agreement to be in writing.

Like a sole proprietorship, there is no state filing requirement for a general partnership, as the business structure will automatically be classified as such for as long as the business partnership exists. With this type of business structure, all partners can be held personally liable for the business's liabilities.

Owners of partnerships that would like to remove their personal liability from the business partnership, must file with the state to classify their partnership either as a limited partnership or a limited liability partnership.

A limited partnership has one general partner with unlimited personal liability while the remaining partners only have limited personal liability. A limited liability partnership, or LLP, offers limited personal liability to all partners in the partnership.

Since this type of business structure requires more than one person to be classified as a partnership, you will be hard pressed to find travel advisors who set up their travel companies as partnerships.

Corporation

Corporations, sometimes referred to as C corps, are a business structure with a legal entity separate from its owners. Corporations are created by filing a certificate of formation with the state. Though a corporation provides the highest protection from personal liability to its owners, the cost to create and continually operate this type of business structure is much higher than the previously listed structures.

Additionally, corporations are required to keep more extensive records, file additional reports, follow more stringent operating requirements, and in some cases, are taxed twice on their earnings. Due to their increased cost and intricate upkeep requirements, it is extremely uncommon for travel advisors to choose a corporation as the business structure for their travel company.

Business Structure Notes

- If you elect to utilize a business structure that requires a state or local county filing, be aware that the information you put on that filing (specifically the business's address) will be viewable by the general public and advertisers. If your travel company's business address also happens to be your personal home address, there are alternatives available to you to help keep your home address private. One option is to utilize a business mailbox address service. Note that it is best to use a business mailbox that has a true address service and not a P.O. box, as some travel suppliers do not support P.O. boxes.

- Classifications, such as S Corporation and Nonprofit, are tax statues that can be utilized by various business structures.

- Wait to choose a business structure until after you have met with a professional business attorney and accountant who specializes in business structures. Though you can convert to a different business structure after your initial filling, some states have restrictions, specific procedures, and tax events, when a change is made. Competent professionals can help you make the right decision the first time and avoid pitfalls and complications when modifying business structures.

Requesting An Employer Identification Number

After your business structure has been selected, the next step is to file for an Employer Identification Number (EIN) issued by the Internal Revenue Service (IRS). Your business may not legally be required to possess an EIN. However, if you would like to open a business checking account or credit card in the name of the business, the bank will normally require a business tax identification number.

You can obtain an business EIN, free of charge, directly from the online IRS website.

Licensing

Thankfully, for those based in the United States, there is no federal licensing mandate required for professional travel advisors. However, there are four U.S. states that require a seller of travel licenses.

As of the date this book is published, California, Florida, Hawaii, and Washington require a state seller of travel license for travel advisors and travel agencies, under certain circumstances. Since regulations consistently change, and laws are routinely updated, this guidebook will not list the current state codes as they can quickly become outdated.

Generally, if any of the following apply, you may need a state seller of travel license:

- You reside or operate your travel business in one of the four mentioned states.

- Your clients reside in one of the four mentioned states.

- Your clients are traveling to one of the four mentioned states.

- You solicit your professional services in one of the four mentioned states.

Some states will also recognize the difference between a travel advisor utilizing a host and a stand-alone agency. This helps provide exemptions and relief to independent contractors, as long as certain conditions are met. For travel advisors and travel agencies that are required to obtain a state seller of travel license, there are two common prerequisites states require to be eligible to apply:

- Normally, if your company was not formed in and does not reside in the state you are seeking a seller of travel license from, you will be required to register your travel company as a foreign entity with the state. Additionally, some states will require a local state mailing address. For those who do not plan on having an in-state location or address, there are registered agent services allowing you to create an local state address that is continually monitored.

- If the state requires a seller of travel bond with the application, you will be required to purchase the required bond amount through a surety bond provider.

Chapter Summary

Business Formation & Licensing Checklist

1. Pick a business name and verify its availability.

2. Choose a business structure and file paperwork if required.

3. Request an EIN from the IRS.

4. Determine if you are required to have a state seller of travel license.

5. If a state seller of travel license is needed:

   I. File or confirm business registration with the associated state.

   II. Purchase seller of travel bonds if required.

   III. Apply for the state seller of travel license.

Business Structure Quick Reference Sheet

Business Structure	Liability	Tax Treatment	Owner
Sole Proprietorship	Unlimited Personal Liability	Personal Tax	One Person
Limited Liability Company (LLC)	Owners Not Personally Liable	Personal Tax or Corporate Tax	One or More Persons
Partnerships	Unlimited Personal Liability (Not Including LLP)	Personal tax	Two or More Persons
Corporation	Owners Not Personally Liable	Corporate tax	One or More Persons

3

Thankfully, in the travel advising profession, there are endless amounts of training opportunities available for advisors looking to increase their knowledge, experience, and expertise. To make things even better, advisors are able to tailor their education to exactly what they would like to learn, and when they would like to learn it. This means that you are able to set the curriculum and your desired training pace to match your learning style and speed.

In addition to general knowledge training, there are a variety of certificate programs, certification courses, and accolade designations available to help showcase your advisor and travel expertise.

Below are the seven main providers of training for professional travel advisors:

- Suppliers
- Travel Industry Education Companies
- Tourism Destination Marketing Organizations
- Accreditation Organizations
- Professional Industry Associations
- Consortia
- Employers

Supplier Training

Supplier training is training offered by a specific brand or company that will educate you on the following:

<u>Travel Products They Offer</u>

- Accommodation Categories
- Class of Service Options
- Spa Services and Fitness Classes
- Tours, Activities, and Excursions
- Restaurants and Dining Venues
- Meal Plans and All-Inclusive Packages
- Property and Ship Overviews
- Amenities
- Locations and Itineraries
- Seasonal Availability, If Not Open Year Round
- Special Events (Groups, Weddings, Corporate)
- Goods and Services

<u>Operations and Procedures</u>

- How Bookings Can Be Made (Phone, Email, In Person, Travel Advisor Online Portal, Public Customer Facing Online Portal)

- How Far in Advance Reservations Can Be Made and When Booking Windows Close

- Accepted Methods of Payment (Local Cash Currency, International Cash Currency, Debit Card, Credit Card, Check)

- Deposit Requirements, If Full Payment Is Not Required at Time of Booking

- Mandatory Fees Not Included in Main Booking Total (Resort, Gratuity, Local Tax)

- Surcharges (Smoking, Pet, Valet, Parking, Wi-Fi, Early Check-In, Late Check-Out, Currency Conversion/Foreign Transaction)

Policies for Guests

- Dress Code
- Baggage Loss or Damage
- Accessibility
- Pregnancy
- Age Requirements
- Alcohol
- Noise
- Identification Requirements
- Curfews
- Safety and Security
- Codes of Conduct
- Occupancy
- Prohibited Items

Online Advisor Portal

- How to Utilize the Quoting and Booking Tools
- How to Setup and Edit Advisor Profiles
- Where to Locate Latest Promotions
- Where to Find Sales Reps and Contacts
- How to Order Marketing Material
- How to Submit Commission Inquiries
- Where to Find Social Media Assets
- How to Sign Up for Email Updates
- How to Request Client Gifts
- How to Create a Group, Charter, or Event

Not every travel supplier will offer an advisor portal. Generally, the larger the company, the more likely they are to have a dedicated advisor portal. The most common way for suppliers to offer training is through an online portal. Select suppliers will also offer in-person training.

Below are brief examples of the types of courses and training opportunities that are available online and in-person:

Online

Suppliers that offer online training generally have both an initial and recurrent training program with predesigned courses. Initial training is in-depth, detailed information that you are being taught for the first time. Recurrent training is follow-up training that is normally offered annually to keep your knowledge current and to notify you of any updates or changes that the supplier has made over the past year.

These online supplier courses and training modules are always offered free of charge to the advisor. Additionally, select suppliers will offer webinars and one-on-one online training sessions to advisors who are looking to increase their knowledge and drive more bookings to said supplier.

In-Person

In-person training offerings with suppliers can vary depending on the travel sector. Hotels and resorts, for example, will normally offer property inspections and host advisor events. Cruise lines will normally offer ship inspections when docked, familiarization trips on select itineraries, seminars at sea, as well as host training sessions at conferences and trade shows.

Normally, in-person training events incur some sort of cost, as you are required to travel to the various training locations.

Accolades and Certificates

Suppliers across the industry, will offer accolades and completion of training certificates to advisors. They can be displayed and viewed by clients, both online and in person. This includes printable certificates, email signature icons, and digital images that can be added to your website or social media pages.

Training Rewards

There are a handful of suppliers, especially in the cruise sector, that will offer training rewards after completing their initial online courseware. These rewards can be: bonus commission on future bookings, discounts for advisor sailings, or gifts that can be applied to a client's reservation.

Supplier Training Summary

Generally, online initial courseware programs can take anywhere between one and sixty hours to complete, depending on the supplier's size and the amount of total products it has to offer. Some of the lengthier programs will also have training tiers that differentiate the various levels of training completed.

Travel Industry Training (Education Companies)

Travel industry education companies offer both free and paid training opportunities to travel advisors. Normally, these companies operate almost exclusively online, with all training being offered digitally. The following types of training are available from industry education companies:

Certification Courses

- Certified Travel Associate (CTA)
- Certified Travel Counsellor (CTC)
- Certified Travel Industry Executive (CTIE)

Destination Training

- Continent, Country, or City Specific
- Polar (Arctic and Antarctic)
- Activity-Based (Skiing, Surfing, Hiking)

Specialized Market Training

- Luxury
- Wellness
- Wedding
- Honeymoon
- Corporate
- Group
- Safari
- Expedition

General Travel Business Courses

- Travel Advisor Taxes
- Business Planning and Career Development
- Global Distribution System (GDS)
- Branding and Marketing
- Website Creation and SEO

Travel Industry Training Summary

Travel industry training provided by education companies offer a great mix of certificate programs, certification courses, and accolade designations. For advisors looking to increase their knowledge of a specific market serviced by multiple suppliers, these (travel advisor) education companies provide the desired courseware so you are not limited to the information issued by just a single supplier.

Tourism Destination Marketing Organizations

Tourism destination marketing organizations, also known as Destination Marketing Organizations (DMOs), are organizations that promote a particular location as an appealing travel or tourist destination. These types of organizations can be centered around entire countries or even a local town.

Normally, training from these organizations will include a mix of the following:

- Top Sites to See
- Best Places to Dine
- How to Get Around
- Popular Tours and Activities
- Finest Accommodations for Each Star Class
- Safety and Security Precautions
- Accepted Methods of Payment and Currency
- Airport Maps Showcasing Direct Flight Options
- Promotions and Offers from Local Suppliers

These organizations are the best place to go for training when a client asks for recommendations in a certain area. Here, you are able to increase your destination expertise with up-to-date information you can count on.

Tourism Destination Marketing Organizations Summary

Training provided by DMOs allows advisors to become location experts and offer quality proposals to travelers.

Accreditation Organization Training

Accreditation organizations offer a variety of training and certification courses, in addition to issuing industry credentials.

Certification Courses

- Certified Cruise Counsellor (CCC)
- Accredited Cruise Counsellor (ACC)
- Master Cruise Counsellor (MCC)
- Elite Cruise Counsellor (ECC)
- Travel Agency Executive (TAE)

Destination Training

- Global Geography

Specialized Market Training

- Groups
- Luxury

General Travel Business Courses

- Client Loyalty
- Groups
- Customer Relationship Management
- Global Distribution System (GDS)
- Social Media Strategy

Accreditation Organization Training Summary

Accreditation organizations set the industry standard when it comes to training provided to advisors. Suppliers communicate with these organizations frequently so that both parties can get the maximum benefit from each other.

Though most accreditation training comes with a cost, if you or your host agency is a member of a consortium, it may provide a number of complimentary accreditation training courses each year.

Additionally, the in-person conferences hosted by accreditation organizations are the most popular advisor conferences in the industry. If you are looking to take some of the best in-person classes or network with like-minded professionals, these are some of the best events to attend.

Professional Industry Association Training

Training opportunities will vary from association to association. There are ample in-person and online options available to advisors, both on a paid and complimentary basis.

Certification Courses

- Certified Travel Specialist (CTS)
- Certified Medical Tourism Professional (CMTP)
- Sports Tourism Strategist (STS)
- Certified Student Travel Professional (CSTP)
- Certified Student Travel Organization (CSTO)
- Verified Travel Advisor (VTA)
- Global Travel Professional (GTP)
- Certified Tour Professional (CTP)

Specialized Market Training

- Business Travel and Meetings Management
- Self-Guided Tour Creation
- Faith-Based Travel
- Special Interest Groups

General Travel Business Courses

- Best Practices
- Building Client Trust
- Travel Agency Regulatory Compliance
- Professional Fees

- Fraud and Scam Prevention
- Identifying Human Trafficking
- Negotiations
- Digital Marketing
- Travel Podcasting
- Customer Service
- Consumer Protection
- Ethics

Professional Industry Association Training Summary

Due to the extremely large number of professional organizations that exist in the industry, there are countless training opportunities available to advisors (from these associations). Additionally, with each organization's unique focus, there are a variety of uncommon training courses that will not be offered by any other training provider.

Consortium Training

Consortium training can be grouped into two main categories:

- Consortium Operational Training (learning about the consortium booking portal, how to navigate the website, and the location of all of the resources you are looking for)

- Standard Industry Training (specialized market training, certification courses, and general travel business courses)

Since consortia are such large organizations that are connected with suppliers, vendors, agencies, advisors, accreditation organizations, and professional organizations, the amount of content and resources they provide can be overwhelming at the beginning.

In addition to the abundance of information and training on the consortia online portals, these companies will routinely offer in-person member events in order to meet suppliers and learn about their offerings, as well as provide courses and seminars on highly requested topics.

Consortium Training Summary

Though there are only a handful of consortia to choose from, these organizations are powerhouses for information and training all across the industry. Learning about all the benefits these groups have to offer for your travel company is key to maximizing your earnings.

Employer Training

Employer training will vary from company to company and can include a combination of the following:

- Company Specific Policies and Procedures
- Detailed Goods and Services Product List
- Customer Service
- General Travel Knowledge Courses
- Sales Basics
- Troubleshooting and Emergency Response
- Booking Portal Overviews and Instruction

Employer Training Summary

Generally, your employers want to train you to be an expert with the products they offer and would like you to have at least a basic understanding of other travel-related topics, so that you can properly communicate with customers and coworkers.

On top of training provided directly by the employer, the company may provide reimbursement or require attendance to industry conferences and events.

Personal Experience & Firsthand Travel Knowledge

Personal experience and firsthand knowledge is a different kind of education that you normally have to equip yourself with. This type of training was left off the list of entities that supply training at the beginning of the chapter, as this method of learning is based on your personal knowledge. This type of training is in complete contrast to previous types of training where learning is based on what someone else is telling you.

In my opinion, this is one of the best ways to learn. In addition to learning from observation, you are also able to learn from personal actions, encounters, and even mistakes. Though I am all for avoiding costly mistakes as much as humanly possible, the reality of life is that people will make mistakes. As long as you can learn from them and avoid repeating the same ones over and over again, you will be able to gain valuable knowledge from your past errors.

One of my biggest reasons for loving this type of learning is that you are able to use trial and error to see what works best for you. Since every advisor is different, the way you market and brand yourself, the services you offer, as well as who you want to work with, are all things you have to try out for yourself and find the right fit. Your initial business plan may end up completely different after firsthand experience, with trial and error, in regards to the way you want to do business.

Chapter Summary

There are seven main providers of training for professional travel advisors:

- Suppliers
- Travel Industry Education Companies
- Tourism Destination Marketing Organizations
- Accreditation Organizations
- Professional Industry Associations
- Consortia
- Employers

All entities from these seven categories of providers issue a variety of certificate programs, certification courses, and accolade designations that advisors can use to broaden their knowledge and showcase their expertise.

4

One of the most common questions I get from people interested in becoming professional travel advisors is: what booking rates do travel advisors have access to? This is a hard question to answer in just two or three sentences. In reality, there are hundreds of different available rates that vary by supplier and sector.

Some of these rates are normal rates that the general public has access to, while other rates are only bookable by travel advisors.

In addition to the public and private rates advisors have access to, there are also multiple public and private booking portals that are available to advisors to secure the actual booking. This means that advisors have the choice of making a booking directly with a supplier through their dedicated booking portal or through a variety of third-party vendors.

The following rate code descriptions that are covered in this chapter can be grouped into two main categories: public rates and private rates. The first group of bookable public rates will be listed before the second group of private rates.

The second group of rates that have to be booked by a travel advisor will have the label (Advisor Only) listed to the right of the rate code title.

Rack Rates

Rack rates, also known as the Best Available Rate (BAR) or standard rate, is the advertised rate provided by the supplier without any discounts applied. This is normally the first rate to populate when making a search directly on a supplier's booking website.

These rates are normally offered on a refundable basis, unless booked inside the supplier's cancelation or penalty period. Additionally, in the hotel, tour, and rental car sector, suppliers will typically not charge the selected form of payment until arrival.

Member Rates

Member rates, also known as loyalty associated rates, are rates offered by suppliers with loyalty programs. To incentivize the client to join the supplier's loyalty program, the supplier will normally offer a 5% discount from the rack rate.

It is very common for member rates to have the exact same cancelation and penalty policy as rack rates. In some instances, suppliers will offer a more generous cancelation and penalty policy for member rates.

Prepay Rates

Prepay rates, also known as Advanced Purchase (AP) rates, are rates that require full payment at the time of booking. Ordinarily, these rates are nonrefundable. Due to these two restrictions, suppliers will normally offer a 5-30% discount from the rack rate for clients who are okay with loosing these two benefits.

Standard Discount Rate Qualifiers

Standard discount rate qualifiers are a common set of discount rate codes that are frequently offered by suppliers. Each of the rate qualifiers below requires specific parameters to be met for the traveler to be eligible for the rate.

- Membership Programs: AAA/CAA & AARP
- Senior
- Military
- Airline
- Student
- Bereavement
- Day Use
- Mobile
- Family (Additional Rooms)
- Long-Term Stay

Membership Programs

Paid membership programs, such as the American Automobile Association (AAA), Canadian Automobile Association (CAA), and the American Association of Retired Persons (AARP), partner with suppliers to offer their members discounted rates with travel suppliers.

The discounts these membership programs offer normally range between 5-30% off the standard rack rate. Typically, the biggest discounts will be offered on the higher end rooms and suites.

Senior

The minimum age to qualify for a senior discount will vary by supplier. Generally, clients over 65 years of age will be eligible for a senior discount, if offered by a supplier. Discounts are typically 5-15% below the standard rack rate.

Military

Military rate eligibility will vary by supplier. Some suppliers will offer a discounted rate to active, retired, and veteran status military members. Other suppliers may restrict this rate to active-duty military members only. Generally, suppliers will offer a 5-50% discount from the normal rack rate.

Airline

Airline leisure rate discounts are normally offered to all employees of regularly scheduled air carriers (Part 121 operators). These rates are separate from active crew rate discounts that are reserved exclusively for on-duty crew. Suppliers will generally offer a 15-25% discount from the normal rack rate.

Student

Student discounts are normally available to any person who posses a current college ID card. Some suppliers will limit this discount to students 26 years of age or less. Discounts are typically 5-10% below the standard rack rate.

Bereavement

Bereavement rate availability will vary by both supplier and location. Thankfully, there are suppliers that offer last minute discounted rates for immediate family members who have experienced a recent loss of life. Suppliers will normally offer 10-30% discount from the standard rack rate.

Day Use

Day use rates are gaining popularity among travel suppliers as their availability continues to increase. Typically, suppliers will offer 20-40% off the standard rack rate.

Note that day use rates only offer day use of the room and do not include overnight accommodations. Check-in and check-out times will vary by supplier, though it is very common to see 8 a.m. - 6 p.m. slots available.

Mobile

Mobile rates are discounted rates that some suppliers offer when making a booking through a mobile device. Suppliers will normally offer a 5-20% discount from the normal rack rate.

Family (Additional Rooms)

Additional rooms booked by parents with children sometimes qualify for family discounts, after the first room has been booked at full price or the standard rack rate.

Typically, suppliers will offer 25-50% off of the second, third, and fourth rooms, as long as the occupants are under the age of 18. These rates are normally not available when booking multiple rooms for adult-only occupants.

Long-Term Stay

Long-term stay rates are normally available after four, five, six, or seven night stays. These rates will either provide a discount between 10-40% off, or they will deduct the nightly rates that qualify for a free night.

Typically, the longer the stay means the higher the available discount. Additionally, stays over 30 days may qualify for exemption from taxes.

Promotional Rates

Promotional rates are either regularly scheduled or out-of-the-blue sales rates that are only available for a set period of time. These rates are normally heavily advertised by the supplier during their running periods. If you or a client have signed up to receive promotional emails from the supplier, this would be the time they would send out an email alerting you of the discounted rates.

Some promotional events will provide rates over 50% below the standard rack rate, while others will normally offer anywhere between 20-30% off of the current rack rate.

Packaged Rates (One Supplier)

Packaged rates that are offered by a single supplier are rates that include standard accommodation just like the regular rack rate does, while also including additional goods and services offered by the same supplier. Below are a few examples of items a supplier could elect to include in a packaged rate:

- Park and Fly Package
- Valet Parking
- Spa Credit
- Dinning Credit or Plan (Half-Board, Full-Board)
- Drink Vouchers
- Bonus Points
- Club or Lounge Access
- Amenity Gifts (Champagne, Chocolate, Flowers)

Typically, supplier packaged rates are 5-30% higher than the standard rack rate, depending on the value of the additional goods and services.

Packaged Rates (Multiple Suppliers)

Packaged rates from multiple suppliers, also known as bundled rates, are packages that combine the goods and services offered by more than one supplier into a single rate. This means that you are able to book a single rate that could include any of the following:

- Airfare
- Hotel/Accommodations
- Rental Car
- Tours/Activities
- Cruise Fare
- Train Fare
- Ground Transportation Fare

Packaged rates normally can be mixed and matched with the amount of different sectors you would like to include. This means that you can custom build the packaged rate as long as there are a minimum of two different suppliers used.

Price Match Rates

Price match rates are rates advisors and clients request from the supplier to match a lower rate found online that is not listed directly on the supplier's website. Sometimes lower rates are listed on third-party booking websites, also referred to as Online Travel Agencies (OTAs). When this occurs, suppliers will sometimes offer the option to submit a rate matching request.

As an added bonus, some suppliers will have an additional discount or reward if the matching rate is approved, thus, lowering the rate an additional 10-20% below the matched rate.

Group and Block Rates

Group and block rates are rates normally available to parties that need more than 10 rooms per booking. These rates typically have to be booked through the group sales department. Discounts will vary depending on the size of the group and normally range between 10-40% below the standard rack rate.

Discount Rates (Advisor Only)

Discounted standard rates or rates better than BAR, are available from select suppliers to travel agencies that have either an associated consortium membership or preferred agency status directly with the supplier. These discounted rates are not available to the public and are required to be made by the agency.

Normally these rates will be between 5-20% below the standard rack rate.

Net Rates (Advisor Only)

Net rates are the lowest standard rates available from the supplier that do not include commission. These rates are typically 10-30% below the standard rack rate and do not offer any compensation to the advisor.

Rack Plus Benefits Rates (Advisor Only)

Rack plus benefits rates are standard rack rates with zero discount, but include complementary value adds for clients. Suppliers may provide these rates to all agencies or may restrict them to a select group of preferred agencies.

These rates can include any of the following:

- Food and Beverage Credit
- Property/Resort Credit
- Early Check-In
- Late Check-Out
- Upgrade
- Welcome Amenity

Consortium Rates (Advisor Only)

Consortium rates are similar to rack plus benefits rates with two minor differences. The first being that the availability of these rates is limited to members of the consortium. The second being that additional discounts can be applied on top of the benefits offered. In this case, you may be able to book a consortium rate that offers a 30% discount below rack, as well as the value adds listed above.

Markup Rates (Advisor Only)

Markup rates, also know as rate choice, are rates the travel advisor sets that are above either the net rates or the BAR. Markups are an advisor's tool to create additional commissions for bookings, if so desired. If suppliers offer a pre-set markup rate, they will normally give options for rates that match 15%, 20%, and 25% commission levels.

Corporate/Custom Rates (Advisor Only)

Custom and corporate rates require contracts and negotiations with supplier sales teams. After a custom rate is created, it can be booked for the eligible parties. Normally these rates will be more than 10% below the standard rack rate and may have additional benefits or value adds attached, depending on the contract.

Travel Advisor Rate (Advisor Only)

Travel advisor rates are rates reserved for travel advisor travel only and cannot be booked for clients. Some suppliers may require travel advisors to complete their online supplier training courses or meet minimum booking quotas before being given access to advisor rates. Discounts will vary by sector and supplier, and range anywhere between 10-90% below the standard rack rate.

Booking Portals

In addition to the variety of rate choices listed above, travel advisors also have a variety of booking methods available to make and secure a reservation.

Below are common portals available to advisors:

- Supplier
- Consortia
- Travel Vendor
- Global Distribution System (GDS)

Supplier Portals

Supplier portals are booking engines that are available to book goods and services offered by that particular supplier only. All bookings made via this method are considered direct bookings, which award the traveler with a variety of benefits not offered to third-party bookings.

Below is a short list of direct booking benefits:

- Brand Status Recognition and Benefits (if a membership or loyalty program is offered)

- Membership Points and Miles Accruals for Future Free Travel Redemptions (if a membership or loyalty program is offered)

- Guest Covered by Supplier Cancelation and Change Policies

- In-Person Customer Service

- Elevated Guest Experience (priority upgrades and amenities)

Consortium Portals

Consortium portals are booking engines that are available to members of a consortium. These portals may offer both direct and third-party booking options with suppliers.

Travel Vendor Portals

Travel vendor portals are booking engines that belong to a consolidator/wholesaler, Online Travel Agency (OTA), or vacation package company. These portals normally only offer advisors third-party booking options.

Global Distribution System (GDS) Portals

There are a handful of companies that offer advisors access to GDS booking portals. This booking system was actually created in the 1960s and is still in use today, especially in the corporate world of travel.

Chapter Summary

Professional travel advisors have access to a variety of public and private rates:

- Rack
- Member
- Prepay
- Standard Discount Qualifiers
- Promotional
- Packaged (One Supplier)
- Packaged (Multiple Suppliers)
- Price Match
- Group and Block
- Discount (Advisor Only)
- Net Rates (Advisor Only)
- Rack Plus Benefits (Advisor Only)
- Consortia (Advisor Only)
- Markup (Advisor Only)
- Corporate/Custom (Advisor Only)
- Travel Advisor (Advisor Only)

Advisors also have access to multiple booking portals to secure a reservation:

- Supplier
- Consortium
- Travel Vendor
- Global Distribution System (GDS)

5

Two of the top questions that aspiring travel advisors normally ask are: how do travel advisors get paid and what is the expected amount of income they can earn?

The answer to the first question is definitively easy to answer for everyone. Travel advisors can be paid in the following four ways:

- Paid a salary or wage by an employer.

- Paid a fee by a client.

- Paid a commission directly by a supplier.

- Paid a commission from a host agency.

The answer to the second question is not as easy to answer, as that number will vary from person to person. If the travel advisor is employed, his or her income will be controlled by his or her employer. If the travel advisor is charging fees to clients, that level of income will be determined by the advisor. If the advisor is earning a commission from a supplier or host agency, that level of income will be determined by commission percentages, the type of bookings made, and the total amount of bookings the advisor makes each year.

In the world of travel advisor commissions, there are a wide variety of commission rates, overrides, incentives, bonuses, credits, promotions, and rewards that are available to advisors. Knowing all of the different income options that are available can drastically increase the income potential for advisors.

Below, you will find a handful of different commission types, with brief explanations and examples.

Base Commission

Base commission, or minimum commission rate, is the lowest guaranteed commission percentage offered by a particular supplier for a commissionable booking. This percentage will vary from supplier to supplier. However, for majority of the industry, 10% is the most common base commission rate.

Consortium Associated Base Commission

Consortium associated base commission rates are elevated base commission rates for travel agencies that are a part of a consortium. For example, a supplier may normally offer a base commission rate of 10% to all travel agencies and offer a 12% base commission rate to travel agencies that are members of a particular consortium.

Agency Production Tiers (Per Supplier)

Some suppliers will offer agency commission production tiers. In short, the more bookings the travel agency makes with the individual supplier, the higher the commission percentage the agency and travel advisors will receive. Below are examples of a supplier production tier chart.

Total Agency Bookings With Specific Supplier	Base Commission Tier
$0 - $15,000	10%
$15,001 - $50,000	12%
$50,001 - $100,000	14%
$100,001 - $200,000	16%
$200,001 - $500,000	18%
$500,001 - $1,000,000	20%
> $1,000,000	25%

Suppliers can also offer separate production tiers for consortium associated agencies.

Total Agency Bookings With Specific Supplier	Base Commission Tier (Consortium)
$0 - $15,000	12%
$15,001 - $50,000	14%
$50,001 - $100,000	16%
$100,001 - $200,000	18%
$200,001 - $500,000	20%
$500,001 - $1,000,000	25%
> $1,000,000	30%

Supplier Enhanced Commission (Rate Choice)

When booking travel for a client, there are normally hundreds of different bookings rates to choose from. If offered by the supplier, the travel advisor can select from various rates that directly correlate to increased commission levels. In the example below, you can see that the advisor can raise the nightly rate above the standard $200 a night level to earn an enhanced commission.

Note that the bonus commission is correlated dollar for dollar with rate increase. So if the advisor elected to book the $230 nightly rate which is $30 more expensive than the standard, they would receive $30 extra in commission per night.

Nightly Rate	Commission Percentage	Standard Commission	Bonus Commission
$200	10% of $200	$20	$0
$210	10% of $200	$20	$10
$220	10% of $200	$20	$20
$230	10% of $200	$20	$30

Supplier Offered Promotional Commission

Generally, promotional commission is not offered 24/7 and is provided either on a seasonal or special offer basis. This type of additional commission usually has a predetermined offer period. For example: make any booking in the next 90 days to qualify for 10% bonus commission. This means that regardless of what your current commission level is with a supplier, you would be able to add 10% to each qualified booking.

Supplier offered bonus commission could also be offered on a cash amount basis instead of a percentage, especially for high-end and luxury bookings. For example: make any booking in the next 90 days and receive $1,000 in extra commission per booking.

Supplier Offered Training Bonus Commission

Specifically in the cruise sector, suppliers will typically offer bonus commission after travel advisors complete their training program and making a successful booking. Normally, this is a set cash bonus and not percentage-based.

Consortium Bonus Commission

In addition to negotiating increased base commission rates with suppliers, consortia also have the opportunity to offer additional bonus commissions to their members. These bonuses can be both percentage-based or cash amount-based, just like supplier offered bonus commissions. However, these supplier bonuses would only be accessible by members of the consortium.

Overrides

Some suppliers that offer a wide range of products will offer commission overrides on their higher end rooms and suites. This means that if you booked a top level room like the penthouse suite, the supplier may pay a higher commission level, say 20%, compared to 10% for other standard rooms at the same property.

Bonus Commissions (Supplier Rewards)

Just like loyalty programs reward travelers for their continued business by issuing points and miles that can be used for future stays with the associated brand, some suppliers will offer travel advisor rewards programs as an additional incentive to make bookings with their brands.

Some supplier reward programs will issue cash or cash equivalents, like gift cards, while other programs will offer travel credits or free travel with the brand. Normally, these programs require a double-digit number of bookings before being able to cash out rewards earnings.

Groups

When putting together a group booking, there are two separate types of group related commissions that can be offered. The first type is group enhanced, or override commission, and is an elevated rate compared to base commission. In this scenario, a supplier may pay a 10% commission rate for a single booking and pay 15% for all bookings contained in a group.

The second type of group related commission is a Trip Credit (TC) or Tour Conductor Credit (TCC). These types of commissions are normally an averaged fare from bookings in the group and are issued on top of the base or group commission rate.

TC & TCC Example:

You book the following 10 rooms for a group traveling together on the same itinerary. Some members of the group booked the cheapest rooms, some booked middle of the road rooms, and others booked higher end suites.

Room 1: Price Per Room $3,000.00

Room 2: Price Per Room $3,000.00

Room 3: Price Per Room $4,500.00

Room 4: Price Per Room $4,500.00

Room 5: Price Per Room $5,500.00

Room 6: Price Per Room $5,500.00

Room 7: Price Per Room $10,000.00

Room 8: Price Per Room $10,000.00

Room 9: Price Per Room $10,000.00

Room 10: Price Per Room $15,000.00

Group Booking Total: $71,000.00

Group Average Room Cost: $7,100.00

If a supplier offered a 10:1 TC or TCC for group bookings, then the following commission payout would occur:

- The base commission, or elevated group base commission, would be issued on the $71,000.00 total. In this scenario, if the group base commission was 15%, there would be $10,650 in commission due on the total booking amount.

- Since the supplier offers one TC or TCC per 10 rooms, this group booking would qualify for one trip credit. In this scenario, the average of the 10 bookings within the group is $7,100.00, which results in a $7,100.00 trip credit due.

- After combining the group TC or TCC with the group base commission, this group booking would earn $17,750 in total commissions. This results in the advisor capturing a 25% commission off of the $71,000.00 booking total.

Local Tourism Rewards

Select country, state, and city tourism marketing companies will offer travel advisors rewards for logging qualifying bookings in their associated rewards portals. These rewards are normally cash or cash equivalents, like gift cards and local travel credits.

Normally, double-digit booking amounts are required to redeem for free travel or cash rewards.

Do Advisors Need to Register for Commissions?

In short: it depends. Travel agencies have to register with each individual supplier, as well as the commission processing companies. Individual advisors do not have to register with suppliers as their personal credentials are not eligible for commission.

So, if you are an advisor that is utilizing a host agency, you are in luck as the host agency will take care of all the supplier registrations. However, if you are starting your own agency, you will be required to register with each supplier one by one. This can be an extremely time consuming process as there are thousands of suppliers you can register with. Registration normally requires the following:

- IRS W9 Form
- Completed Agency Application Form
- Company Letterhead with Agency Information
- Copy Of Agency Accreditation Certificate
- Electronic Banking Details

Agency Letterhead Example:

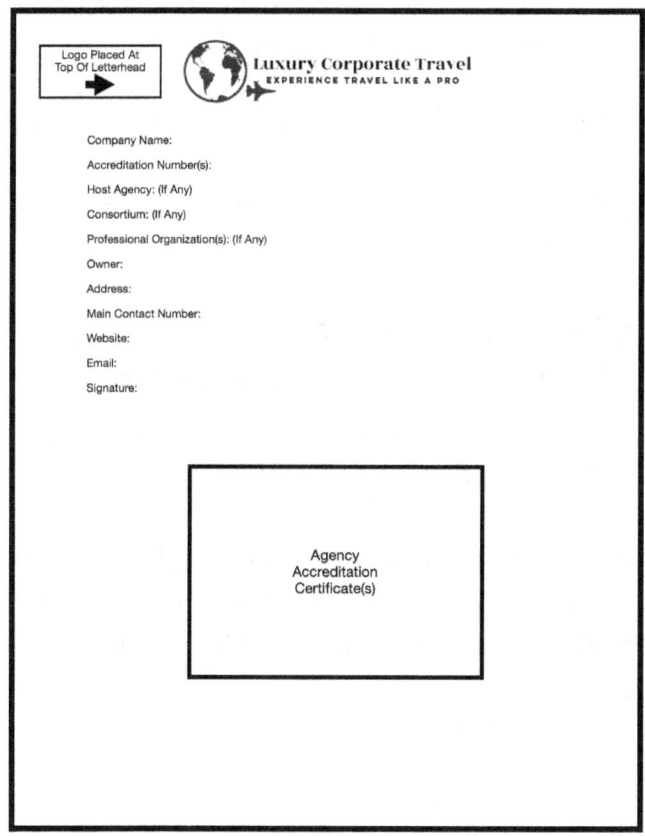

My recommendation is to not wait to register, as some agency onboardings can take weeks. If you are an individual advisor and find a supplier that your host agency is not currently registered with, let them know as soon as possible so they can begin the registration process and have the account set up by the time you are ready to book a client.

When Are Commissions Issued?

This answer will vary from supplier to supplier. Generally, suppliers will issue commission after the reservation has been completed. In some instances, cruise lines will issue commission after final payment is made, even before the trip begins.

How Is Commission Processed for Travel Agencies?

Commissions are generally processed from one of four sources:

- Directly from Supplier
- Travel Agency Commission Settlement (TACS)
- ONYX CenterSource
- Paymode-X

Note that if you are an individual advisor utilizing a host agency, your host will take care of commission processing registration, discrepancies, and inquiries for missing commission.

Are There Any Offsets to Commissions?

Offsets to commissions, and variables that reduce commission amounts, are most commonly currency conversion fees, supplier processing fees, and physical check processing fees. These fees are normally less than 5% of the total commission amount.

Are There Any Instances Where All or Part of a Booking Is Non-Commissionable?

Yes. Generally this will occur for one of two reasons:

1. The rate selected for booking is identified as non-commissionable; or

2. If any part of the booking has taxes, supplemental charges, or Non-Commissionable Fees (NCFs), those amounts are excluded from commission totals.

NCFs exist in the cruise sector. NCFs normally include items such as port charges, local taxes, and immigration cost.

How Are Suppliers Able to Pay Commissions to Advisors Without Increasing the Cost of the Booking?

In short: employees are very expensive. Most suppliers will have large booking and customer service departments with around the clock salaried employees who advise clients, create and service bookings, as well as provide customer service support. No matter how many bookings the employee creates, the supplier will shell out a full salary, employment taxes, employee benefits like healthcare, retirement savings, paid vacation time, sick time, and supplemental insurance policies, as long as the employee is on the clock.

These costs are already built into the rate offered by the supplier. So, instead of covering all of the expenses associated with an employee, the supplier issues a commission to the advisors for creating and servicing the booking. This is how advisors are able to earn commissions on bookings without an increased rate for the client.

How Much Can Travel Advisors Make?

This is one of my favorite questions to answer. The short answer is that it depends on each person. Normally, I am asked this question by advisors who are not looking to work as an employee for a company and want to be an independent advisor who books travel when and where he or she pleases.

Since these types of advisors are able to choose how often they are booking travel, who they are booking travel for, and what types of bookings they want to make, they are in control of how much income they can capture. This also makes it hard to give a hard number to someone interested in becoming a professional travel advisor, as no advisor will have the exact same bookings as another.

To help give a better ballpark figure, the first question you need to answer is the following:

Do you plan on booking travel full-time or part-time?

For those that answer part-time, I like to provide a few per trip commission examples. These show how much you would typically make per booking and is an easy to use tool to estimate income if you are only planning on making a handful of bookings per year.

$2,000 is normally the amount for a budget one week family trip to somewhere in North America. $8,000 is the common middle-class one week family or couples trip outside of the United States. $20,000 is the common week long cost for an upper-middle-class trip — typically a luxury cruise or five-star resort outside of the United States.

Trip Cost	10% Commission	15% Commission	20% Commission
$2,000	$200	$300	$400
$8,000	$800	$1,200	$1,600
$20,000	$2,000	$3,000	$4,000

If a part-time advisor is booking trips for friends and family and only expects to book an estimated 15 trips per year, he or she can use the estimates above to help get an idea of his or her potential income. If all of the booked trips are for budget travelers and the selected supplier only issues 10% commission, the advisor would only earn $3,000 a year. On the other end of the scale, if they planned honeymoon trips part-time and still only booked 15 trips a year, they would earn $30,000 a year at a 10% commission rate.

For advisors who are interested in working full time and are looking to make numerous amounts of bookings year-round, I like to provide a chart with annual booking amounts to help gauge the potential income.

Total Annual Bookings	Averaged 10% Commission	Averaged 15% Commission	Averaged 20% Commission
$50,000	$5,000	$7,500	$10,000
$100,000	$10,000	$15,000	$20,000
$200,000	$20,000	$30,000	$40,000
$300,000	$30,000	$45,000	$60,000
$400,000	$40,000	$60,000	$80,000
$500,000	$50,000	$75,000	$100,000
$600,000	$60,000	$90,000	$120,000
$700,000	$70,000	$105,000	$140,000
$800,000	$80,000	$120,000	$160,000
$900,000	$90,000	$135,000	$180,000
$1,000,000	$100,000	$150,000	$200,000
$1,250,000	$125,000	$187,500	$250,000
$1,500,000	$150,000	$225,000	$300,000
$2,000,000	$200,000	$300,000	$400,000
$3,000,000	$300,000	$450,000	$600,000
$5,000,000	$500,000	$750,000	$1,000,000
$10,000,000	$1,000,000	$1,500,000	$2,000,000

If some of the annual booking numbers on that chart seem outrageous, I can assure you they are possible. The following four examples show how, in some cases, just a few clients and bookings can result in significant annual booking and commission amounts.

Example One

Normally, when putting a group trip together, you can work with suppliers who provide overrides and credits on group bookings so that commission levels can routinely exceed 20%.

If you create a single group booking with around 12-15 people, this one booking can account for over $100,000 towards your annual booking amount. If you made just 10 of these types of bookings per year, that would equate to over $200,000 in yearly commissions.

Example Two

You land a corporate account to manage travel for a small business (typically less than 100 employees). If that business has a decent amount of employee travel, it's not uncommon for these types of businesses to accrue over a million dollars in bookings per year without breaking a sweat. At a 10% commission average, that is a minimum of $100,000 in commissions just from one client each year.

Example Three

If one of the services or specializations you offer as an advisor is destination weddings, you have the opportunity to book extremely large groups for both the wedding itself, as well as pre and post accommodations and activities for guests who would like to turn the wedding weekend into an extended vacation.

One wedding with around 100 to 200 guests can exceed $450,000 in total bookings for the event. At a 10% commission average, the advisor would earn $45,000 in commission per wedding.

Example Four

There are a wide range of trips that can generate six-figure booking amounts even when booking for just a a solo traveler or couple. These can be bucket list type of trips, like three weeks in an overwater bungalow in the Maldives or Tahiti, luxury Arctic or Antarctic expedition trips, or even a run-of-the-mill world cruise in a standard cabin.

In this example, just one booking can account for over $100,000 towards an annual booking amount and over $10,000 in commission income.

Chapter Summary

Travel advisors can be paid in the following four ways:

- Paid a salary or wage by an employer.
- Paid a fee by a client.
- Paid a commission directly by a supplier.
- Paid a commission from a host agency.

There are a variety of commission levels, available to advisors, that can vary based on a combination of factors. Generally, most suppliers will set a minimum 10% base commission rate and pay commission after a reservation is completed.

6

Though expenses aren't nearly as fun to plan for as income is, the reality is that expenses will always be an ongoing factor in running your travel company, whether you are an independent advisor or operate your own agency. The only advisors who will not incur any expenses are those who are employed by another company.

For advisors who will operate their own travel business, it can be extremely hard to project what expenses you may incur, especially when entering the industry for the first time.

One of the main reasons expense planning is difficult for travel advisors is because expenses can vary dramatically from one advisor to another, just like commission income can. This means that any data point you find from another advisor or agency could be nowhere near the same as yours, even though you operate in the same field.

The good news is, you get to choose what expenses you want your travel company to incur based on your operations. This helps keep you in control of your total cost.

Though some business expenses are mandatory, while others are optional, one of the biggest factors that will dictate a travel advisor's expected expenses is the advisor's decision to operate his or her travel company under a host agency or manage his or her own agency.

Because cost varies drastically between these two choices, the expected expenses associated with each option are listed separately. Expected independent travel advisor expenses are listed first, followed by expected travel agency expenses later in the chapter.

Each expense example listed in this chapter will contain a brief description followed by an expected cost range. If a cost range begins with $0, that means that the expense example could be optional, thus resulting in zero expenses. It could also mean that there are free or complementary options for that example that do not incur an expense.

For example: the Training & Educational Items expense example has a range from $0 to $1,000+ per year. Because some training is free of charge, the range begins at zero. That being said, there is a long list of paid training options that could add up to well beyond $1,000 each year, if you choose to incur those expenses.

Expected Independent Travel Advisor Expenses

Operating as an independent advisor through a host agency helps reduce both the startup and ongoing cost for your travel company, compared to operating your own agency. Below are common expenses that travel advisors can incur over the course of their business operations:

- Business Formation
- Hosting
- Insurance
- Website/Domain Name
- Conferences/Trade Shows
- Professional Membership(s)
- Training & Educational Items
- Personal Accreditation
- CRM Software
- Advertising/Marketing
- Client Gifts
- Promotional Items
- Familiarization Experiences
- International Phone Plan
- General Business Expenses

Business Formation

When creating your business, there are a variety of costs that can occur during the business structure and formation process.

- Filings with the State (If Required)

- Professional Filing Services (If You Prefer to Have Business Structure Formation Paperwork Completed by Someone Else)

- Consultation & Professional Services (When Working with a Professional Attorney and Accountant)

- Business Address or Registered Agent Service (If You Elect to Use a Mailing Address Other Than Your Home Address)

Range: $0 to $1,000+ Per Year

Hosting

Hosting expenses can vary widely depending on the host agency you select. There are some host agencies that do not charge any sort of hosting fee while others have fees in excess of $5,000 per year. Note that some host agencies will include insurance for advisors in their hosting fee.

Range: $0 to $5,000+ Per Year

Insurance

The two most common types of insurance for travel company owners are: general liability insurance and errors and omissions insurance.

General liability insurance, also referred to as business liability insurance or corporate general liability insurance, is a business insurance that normally covers the following items:

- Bodily Injury (Client Slips & Falls at Your Store)

- Personal Injury (Libel and Slander)

- Property Damage (You Damage a Client's Passport)

- Advertising Injury (Competitor Claims You Copied Their Advertisements)

Errors and Omissions Insurance, also referred to as E&O insurance or professional liability insurance, is a professional business insurance that normally covers the following items:

- Inaccurate Advice (You Tell a Client Their Hotel Has Free Parking by Mistake)

- Negligence (You Fail to Cancel a Reservation before the Penalty Period Begins)

- Errors (You Booked the Wrong Check-Out Date)

- Omissions (You Forget to Tell the Client That His or Her Hotel Will Charge an Additional Resort Fee upon Arrival)

For both types of insurance, policy cost will vary depending on a variety of factors:

How Much Coverage You Would Like

This refers to your total insured amount. If you would like a policy that insures against claims up to half a million dollars, you will pay a lower premium compared to a policy that insures against claims up to five million dollars.

Note that an insurance premium is a monthly, quarterly, semi-annual or annual amount that you pay to the insurance company for the insurance product they underwrite to you.

What You Would Like Covered

Since every advisor will operate differently from another, what one advisor needs covered may not be what another advisor needs covered. Generally, the more you want covered, the higher your premiums will be.

How High of a Deductible Do You Want to Select

A deductible is an amount you are willing to cover yourself before your insurance kicks in. Generally, the higher your deductible, the lower your insurance premiums will be.

Do You Want Any Additional Riders or Add-Ons

Insurance riders are additions to your selected insurance policy. One of the most common riders that travel advisors add to their business policies is a tour operator rider.

The Amount of Travel You Book

Your annual sales volume can affect your insurance premiums. Generally, the higher your sales volumes, the higher your insurance premiums.

The Type of Travel You Book

Not all types of travel carry the same risk. For example, booking refundable domestic only vacations directly with suppliers carries much less risk than booking nonrefundable third-party group bookings to third-world countries.

The State You Are Located In

Though most professional travel advisors operate their business from the comfort of their own home and aren't subject to the same risk as physical brick-and-mortar businesses, insurance premiums can vary from one state to another.

Your Credit Score

Generally, lower credit scores indicate a higher chance of missing a financial obligation, such as an insurance premium payment.

Previous Claims History

If your business has a routine habit of filing insurance claims, typically the insurance provider will increase your premium cost to avoid losses from your account.

Experience Level

Normally, operators with decades of experience are less likely to make costly rookie mistakes than a newcomer has yet to learn from.

Range: $0 to $1,000+ Per Year

Website/Domain Name

If you elect to have an online website for your travel company, the two main parts of the website are: the website host and the website domain.

Website hosts are companies that make your website available to users of the internet. Generally, these companies will offer website building services or build-your-own website platforms that allow you to design your website.

Main factors that determine the cost of a website host are the features they provide to users, such as if you select an ad free host provider or if they allow you to use a custom website domain name.

Website domain, also known as domain name, is the unique address used to access your specific website. This address is what users would type into an internet browser search bar to locate your website.

Generally, custom website domain names can be purchased for less than $20 per year. Additionally, different types of domain extensions will warrant different costs. For example, .com is the most popular domain extension and usually costs more than the following extensions:

- .org
- .net
- .info
- .us
- .shop
- .ai
- .blog

Range: $0-$500+ Per Year

Conferences/Trade Shows

Conferences and trade shows occur throughout the year and can be hosted by accreditation organizations, destination marketing companies, and professional organizations. Generally, admission for these multi-day events ranges between $150-$300 per event.

Note that the expected range listed below is only accounting for event admission cost, without accounting for transportation or accommodation expenses for events outside your local area.

Range: $0 to $1,000+ Per Year

Professional Membership(s)

Cost will vary from association to association. Generally, the more benefits the organization offers to its members, the higher the membership fee. Note that some professional organizations offer a variety of other common business expenses such as insurance, training, and business software, at significantly discounted rates.

Range: $0 to $1,000+ Per Year

Training & Educational Items

There are a variety of training and educational expenses that advisors can elect to purchase in addition to free training offerings:

- Certificate Programs
- Certification Courses
- General Business Training
- Books (like this one!)

Range: $0 to $1,000+ Per Year

Personal Accreditation

Some hosts will require personal accreditation credentials, while others do not. If required, costs normally range between $25 and $150 per accreditation, depending on the consortium affiliation of the host agency.

Range: $0 to $300+ Per Year

Customer Relationship Management (CRM) Software

Customer relationship management software offers a variety of tools to advisors. Though the offerings from each software provider can vary, the following tools are normally included:

- Create Itineraries and Trip Quotes
- Store Client Details
- Trip Calendars and Deadline Reminders
- Credit Card Authorization Forms
- Flight Monitoring
- Lead Management
- Booking Logs

Range: $0 to $500+ Per Year

Advertising/Marketing

Marketing and advertising, both the services you offer as well as supplier trips and destinations, can be done through free or paid marketing methods.

If you elect to do co-op marketing with suppliers to promote their product, generally they will be willing to match marketing funds if your campaign is approved. In theory, you can spend nearly an infinite amount on marketing and advertising. That being said, most advisors will try and maximize their marketing efforts through cost-free platforms such as social media.

Range: $0 to $1,000+ Per Year

Client Gifts

Some suppliers have dedicated gift portals where you can purchase gifts for your clients. These gifts can range from low cost items such as a $10 assortment of chocolates to $300 bottles of champagne. Generally, the more expensive and luxurious the booking, the higher the cost of the gift.

Note that it is not a requirement for an advisor to purchase gifts for clients.

Range: $0 to $1,000+ Per Year

Promotional Items

Promotional items are customized items with your travel company information on them. These items can be travel related products, like a luggage tag or packing cubes, or other useful items that will continually remind clients of your brand.

Range: $0 to $1,000+ Per Year

Familiarization Experiences

Familiarization trips and site visits are a great way to get to know a product very well, especially if you have never experienced it before. Note that the range below does not account for travel to and from familiarization trips and site visits, and only includes the cost associated with the product experience.

Range: $0 to $5,000+ Per Year

International Phone Plan

This business expense is separate from the general business expense list as a majority of U.S. small businesses do not utilize international calls for their day to day operations. As travel advisors, it is a common occurrence to call an international supplier to make or service a booking, as well as complete custom requests through local employees, like the concierge desk.

Note that some calls can be made free of charge via Wi-Fi calling applications and services that do not require cell service for voice or video communications.

Range: $0 to $500+ Per Year

General Business Expenses

Though you may already be paying for some of the items below for your everyday lifestyle, these items can be categorized as business expenses.

- Internet/Wi-Fi
- Computer
- Phone/Cell Phone
- Tax Preparation Services
- Trademark Logo, Name, or Slogan
- Utilities
- Office Supplies
- Business Cards

Range: $0 to $500+ Per Year

Independent Travel Advisor Expenses Summary

As you can see from the previous expense ranges, it is very hard to establish a single average cost that advisors can use to project their expenses. Additionally, the gap from the low side of the scale where advisors have extremely few expenses, to the high side of the scale where advisors have thousands of dollars in expenses, is quite large.

Normally, as businesses expand and bookings increase, it can be expected to see expenses continue to rise as your travel company grows. For many advisors, cost can be minimized at the beginning of their venture and strategically raised as their bookings increase.

Expected Travel Agency Expenses

Travel agencies have the following potential business expenses:

- Business Formation
- Agency Accreditation(s)
- Consortium Membership
- Seller of Travel License
- Physical Location
- Professional Membership(s)
- Conferences/Trade Shows
- Insurance
- CRM Software
- Website/Domain Name
- Training & Educational Items
- Advertising/Marketing
- Client Gifts
- Promotional Items
- International Phone Plan
- Familiarization Experiences
- General Business Expenses

Note that some business expense categories are the same as individual advisors. However, higher expenses can occur for agencies in the same category, as described below.

To avoid repetitive text, only the differences in cost will be listed for the expense categories that were previously defined in the independent travel advisor section.

Business Formation

Travel agencies will typically have multiple business formation filings, due to state seller of travel laws requiring agencies to register as a foreign entity before applying for a seller of travel license. This increased number of filings normally adds $1,000 to $3,000 more in annual filing expenses.

Range: $0 to $5,000+ Per Year

Agency Accreditation(s)

Though individual advisors may or may not need credentials, agencies are required to be accredited. Some agencies will elect for just one accreditation number, while others will pay for multiple accreditations.

Range: $400 to $3,000+ Per Year

Consortium Membership

If an agency elects to join a consortium, annual membership fees will vary from one consortium to another. Generally, the higher the agency sales volumes are, the higher the annual membership fee will be.

Range: $200 to $10,000+ Per Year

Seller of Travel License

The four states that still have seller of travel licenses have variable fees depending on the state. Generally, there can be four different expenses associated with each state's seller of travel license.

1. Seller of Travel Bond
2. Local or Foreign Business Formation Filing
3. Registered Agent Service for Local Address
4. Seller of Travel Application and License

Range: $0 to $5,000+ Per Year

Physical Location

Though brick-and-mortar storefronts are very uncommon in the industry, if an agency chooses to operate a physical location for walk-in customers, cost will vary depending on the location and the current commercial real estate market.

Range: $0 to $50,000+ Per Year

Professional Membership(s)

Most professional organizations have separate membership categories for individuals and for agencies. Generally, membership costs for companies are two to five times higher than the cost of an individual membership.

Range: $0 to $5,000+ Per Year

Conferences/Trade Shows

Conferences and trade shows sometimes charge higher rates to companies over individual attendees. Additionally, some host agencies may provide hosted advisors with free or discounted cost, if included in their agency registration benefits.

Range: $0 to $2,000+ Per Year

Insurance

As a standalone agency, insurance cost can be higher compared to advisors who have access to a group plan, or have their insurance covered by their hosting fee.

Range: $0 to $5,000+ Per Year

Customer Relationship Management (CRM) Software

Customer relationship management software operators may come at a higher cost for agency plans compared to individual plans. Additionally, some host agencies may include this type of software in their monthly hosting fee.

Range: $0 to $1,000+ Per Year

The Following Business Expenses Have No Significant Cost Difference

Website/Domain Name
Range: $0 to $500+ Per Year

Training & Educational Items
Range: $0 to $1,000+ Per Year

Advertising/Marketing
Range: $0 to $1,000+ Per Year

Client Gifts
Range: $0 to $1,000+ Per Year

Promotional Items
Range: $0 to $1,000+ Per Year

International Phone Plan
Range: $0 to $500+ Per Year

Familiarization Experiences
Range: $0 to $5,000+ Per Year

General Business Expenses
Range: $0 to $5,000+ Per Year

Travel Agency Expenses Summary

Just like independent advisor expenses vary from advisor to advisor, travel agency expenses will vary from agency to agency. Typically, larger agencies with higher volumes of bookings can expect a higher level of expenses compared to smaller boutique agencies.

Chapter Summary

No travel company will be the same in regards to expenses. Thankfully, cost can be greatly minimized for individual advisors as they slowly build their client list and increase their booking numbers when first entering the industry.

Travel agency owners are subject to higher operating costs due to mandatory agency accreditation, as well as other agency only expenses, such as consortium memberships.

The general example below is a single expense comparison from an individual advisor to an travel agency, to help visualize the potential difference in operating cost. The following numbers are for demonstration purposes only and do not represent real life data.

Expense	Individual Advisor	Travel Agency
Accreditation(s)	$80	$900
Business Filling(s)	$200	$2,500
Hosting Fee	$400	$0
SOT License(s)	$0	$2,800
Consortium Fee	$0	$4,500
Insurance	$500	$3,000
Website	$400	$400
Conferences	$250	$800
Total Annual Cost	$1,830	$14,900

7

Creating a strong brand and marketing your travel company can help your business in a multitude of ways. Branding involves creating an identity for your company which can be supported by items such as your company name, logo, tagline, website design, and marketing material. Marketing consist of promoting your brand and services to gain interest from travelers.

Before you can market your services, you first need to create your brand. Creating a strong, unique brand may seem like an extremely difficult task as you are essentially creating something that has never existed before. The good news is that creating an identity for your company can be relatively easy if you can pinpoint what you would like your brand's identifying features to be.

To help showcase how this can be done, I will provide a few samples from my company and how I created that brand. Below is a picture of my company logo which includes the company name, tagline, and illustrated design.

The brand I wanted to create revolved around the identity of high-value professional travel services.

The following are features, traits, attributes, and similar words that come to mind for each part of the logo:

Company Name: Luxury Corporate Travel

Luxury

- High Standards
- Superior Quality
- High-End
- Exceptional Service
- Award Winning
- Best Of The Best
- First Class
- Exclusive
- One-of-a-Kind Experience

Corporate

- Professional
- Skilled
- Experienced
- Licensed
- Qualified
- Sense of Authority
- Competent
- Savvy
- Confident
- Decisive
- Dependable

<u>Travel</u>

- Journey
- Trip
- Vacation
- Adventure
- Roam
- Discover
- Relax
- Detach
- Decompress
- Explore

Because I wanted to create an identity for my brand that revolved around high-value professional travel services, the features, traits, and attributes for each word in the company name all reinforce that identity. "Luxury" helped represent high value. "Corporate" helped represent professionalism, and "Travel" helped represent travel services.

Tagline: Experience Travel Like a Pro

"Pro" is short for professional. A Professional can be referred to as someone who is the best at what he or she does. For example, a professional athlete is someone who can play a particular sport better than the general public.

In the tagline's case, I wanted to convey the message that travelers themselves can feel like they are going to experience the best possible way to travel, just like a professional would.

Illustration: Globe & Fighter Jet

<u>Globe</u>

- Visual Representation of Earth
- Countries, Continents, and Places to Travel
- Oceans and Water
- Inspiration
- Knowledge
- Curiosity

<u>Fighter Jet</u>

- Extremely Quick
- Sharp
- Accurate
- Agile
- Protective
- State of the Art

The globe was chosen to help reinforce the travel identity, while the fighter jet was selected to represent precision and the idea that requests are done right the first time of asking.

Note that the color black was selected for the entire logo. Colors can also be associated with variable traits and meanings. Since black reinforces seriousness, luxury, and professionalism, it was the perfect choice to help strengthen the brand identity I was trying to create.

In addition to the logo, the company website and marketing materials were utilized to continue forming the brand identity. I wanted to create a simple and refined design that was free from distractions and exemplified a sense of wonder and professionalism.

To achieve this identity, I elected to use uncluttered landscape photographs and sole attention grabbing items to avoid sensory overload. With a less-is-more concept, viewers are able to think and imagine more, instead of being continually mentally preoccupied by excessive content.

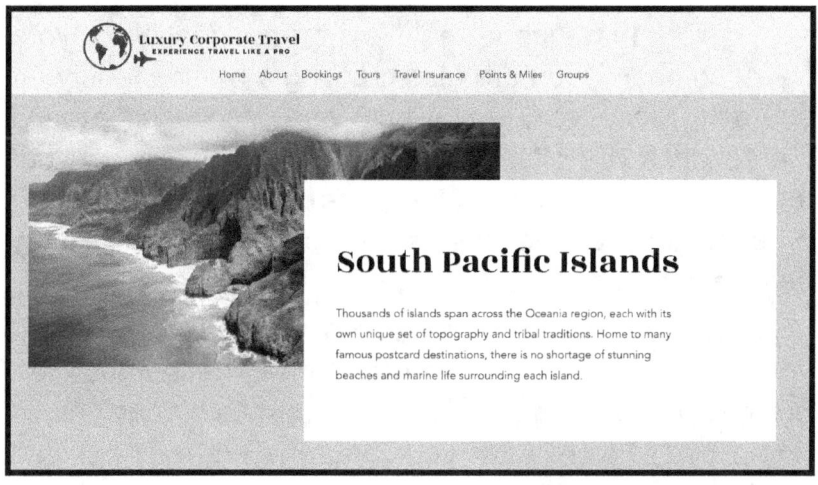

Pictured above: screenshot from the company website.

Pictured to the right: front cover of brochure sent out to travelers.

Brand Example Summary

The following brand identities are represented by the company logo, website, and marketing material:

1. Professional Travel Services (Company Name)
2. Best Possible Experience (Tagline)
3. Curiosity and Preciseness (Illustration Design)
4. Simple and Refined (Website)
5. Wonder and Professionalism (Marketing Material)

Note that when creating a brand identity for your travel company, you are also creating a brand identity for yourself. Since your travel business is focused around the services you offer as a travel professional, how your identity is perceived by others will affect their presumptions of the values, expertise, and skills they believe you possess.

Once you have pinpointed what you would like your brand's identifying features to be, thesauruses are great tools that can be utilized to formulate your unique name and tagline. After your brand is put together and ready to be seen by others, you are ready to begin marketing.

As a refresher, marketing consists of promoting your brand and services to gain interest from travelers. Essentially, marketing is the process of letting people know your business exists. It can be accomplished in a variety of ways. Note that marketing can also be used to remind people about your travel company, if they were previously aware of your services, and entice them to plan a trip.

The following are ways you can market your travel company and the services you provide:

- Word of Mouth
- Client Referrals
- Travel Advisor Listings
- Business Directory Listings
- Creating a Website
- Social Media
- Email
- Direct Mail
- Local Advertising
- Online Advertising
- Online Groups
- Trade Shows/Conferences
- Professional Associations
- Affiliate and Business Partnerships
- In-Person Events

Word of Mouth

Word of mouth is normally the first method of marketing travel advisors utilize. Fundamentally, word of mouth is verbally telling people about your business and what you do. This can be done with people you know extremely well, such as friends and family, or to someone you are meeting for the first time at a social gathering.

Client Referrals

Client referrals are a great way to market your services, as this type of marketing occurs when a previous traveler tells others about your services and all the great things you offer. This may occur without you even knowing or through a dedicated referral program where the traveler is incentivized for sending business in your direction.

Travel Advisor Listings

Travel advisor listings are online directories that include your business name and contact information so that people searching for an advisor can connect with you. Some directories and listing channels will also populate additional information such as personal travel experience or what you specialize in.

Below is a list of organizations that offer online agent listings:

- Consortia
- Accreditation Organizations
- Professional Associations
- Travel Suppliers
- Destination Marketing Companies
- Host Agencies

Business Directory Listings

Business directory listings are similar to travel advisors listings, except they are not tailored specifically to travel advisors. These online directories will have a variety of different business types across a wide range of industries.

Common business directory listings organizations include:

- Chamber of Commerce
- Search Engines
- Private Business Directory Companies

Creating a Website

Creating a custom website allows you to display an expansive amount of marketing material. Websites permit you to provide detailed descriptions about your business, yourself, what you specialize in, and attractive travel destinations.

This allows a traveler to get to know you better, verify your experience, read about your travel history, and see all you have to offer.

Social Media

Most social media companies support both personal and business accounts. This allows you to have an additional account specifically for your business, across all platforms. Many advisors will use these platforms to market eye-catching photos and videos as users are primarily using social media for entertainment.

To make things even easier for the advisor, travel suppliers have social media kits with dedicated captions and approved media assets that the advisor can utilize.

Email

Email marketing can be accomplished by building email lists and sending out mass general marketing material or by targeting specific groups or single clients. Suppliers will also have email assets for advisors, as well as webinar links that can be distributed.

This method of marketing can be a great tool to utilize when a particular supplier is offering a special promotion.

Direct Mail

Direct mail is physical marketing material that is delivered via the mail system. Advisors can utilize supplier and consortium co-op marketing materials that can be customized to show your travel company logo and contact information. Direct mail can be targeted by both location and income level.

Local Advertising

Local advertising is a marketing method used to let local travelers in your area know about your business and services. The following are ways you can advertise in your local area:

- Sponsor a Youth Team or Event
- Charity Functions

- Newspaper Listing
- Flyers
- Community Groups
- Billboards
- Radio
- Phone Book Listing
- Local News Appearance
- Fundraisers

Online Advertising

Online advertising can also be targeted to your local area, though it offers the capability for you to market to travelers all over the world. This is especially helpful when your target client does not reside in your local area. This type of marketing can also be targeted by keywords which allows your marketing material to reach very specific targets.

Online Groups

Online groups are an extremely popular way for travel advisors to market their travel company. You can join existing groups or create your own. Groups allow you to showcase your expertise by answering questions from other members and explain all the benefits you can provide from your services.

The following are common group categories you can seek out, or give inspiration to, if you would like to create your own:

- Location-Based (can be broad such as "visit South Pacific," or very specific such as "Bora Bora five star hotels")

- Supplier Specific (could be for previous guests, review groups, meetup groups for specific itineraries, or question and answer groups)

- Status and Loyalty (these are for guests who have earned a certain level of brand status due to the amount of previous business spent with the brand)

- Small Business (normally these groups are not travel related but offer opportunities to connect with other small businesses with corporate travel needs)

Trade Shows/Conferences

Trade shows and conferences allow you to market your travel company at industry-specific events. These events don't have to be travel related. For example, if you attended a yacht trade show, you could have a booth and market yacht charters offered by suppliers.

Professional Associations

Professional associations offer great networks to market your travel business to both members of the association as well as outside parties that the association interacts and advertises with.

Affiliate and Business Partnerships

Teaming up and partnering with other businesses allows other parties to advocate and promote your services on your behalf. These businesses could also be individuals, such as travel influencers or group organizers.

In-Person Events

In-person events are self-hosted marketing events that allow travel advisors to deliver visual presentations, offer promotional booking incentives, and field questions from travelers. These events are very popular in the cruise sector.

Note that some suppliers will offer co-op funds to help sponsor vacation and cruise nights.

Travel Branded Items

The following are popular travel-related items that can be branded with your company logo and given to potential and repeat travelers:

- Luggage Tags
- Luggage Straps
- Cruise Lanyards
- Bluetooth Luggage Trackers
- Travel Pouches
- Amenity Kits
- Passport Holders
- Travel Adapters

Chapter Summary

Branding involves creating an identity for your company which can be supported by items such as your company name, logo, tagline, website design, and marketing material.

Marketing consists of promoting your brand and services to gain interest from travelers. It is important to market what you want to book, as people will want to book what you are marketing. You are marketing more than just your company and the trips you are able to book. You are marketing yourself and your expertise as well.

You can market your travel company and the services you provide in the following ways:

- Word of Mouth
- Client Referrals
- Travel Advisor Listings
- Business Directory Listings
- Creating a Website
- Social Media
- Email
- Direct Mail
- Local Advertising
- Online Advertising
- Online Groups
- Trade Shows/Conferences
- Professional Associations
- Affiliate and Business Partnerships
- In-Person Events

8

Most travel advisors who create their own travel company naturally want to gain experience, grow their business, and increase their bookings year after year. To successfully accomplish this ambition, advisors must continually perform the following three actions:

1. Set Goals
2. Evaluate Their Performance
3. Take Part in Professional Development

Setting goals helps provide an advisor with a clear direction and continuous motivation. Goals can also serve as a great daily reminder of what your top priorities are while aiding in personal accountability.

Not only is setting goals important, but reviewing your yearly performance allows you to pinpoint where you can improve. If you are falling short of a set goal, being able to identify where a change needs to be made can help put you back on the right track. This also allows you to take a moment and appreciate all of the goals you successfully achieved.

Professional development is another essential component that can be utilized to help achieve your goals. This process encompasses a variety of different methods but focuses on self improvement through continuing education, training, and personal experience.

Including these three actions into your yearly operations can help create a concrete path towards successful growth.

Setting Goals

Setting goals can be one of the most exciting tasks an advisor can perform, as this process allows you to imagine your future self after achieving everything you planned to accomplish. When you can clearly picture yourself in this scenario, your body can produce a small dose of dopamine. This chemical is normally produced by the brain after you feel a sense of accomplishment.

Once this feel-good signal is felt, your natural instinct is to want that same (good) feeling to occur again. Since you can create this feeling just from envisioning what could be, your mind will automatically conceive a natural motivation to repeat this sensation with what can be.

To help increase the probability of achieving your goals and recreating the satisfying sense felt after accomplishment, the following parameters need to be met when creating your goals:

- Documented and Written Down
- Specific and Straightforward
- Measurable With the Capability to Evaluate
- Realistic and Obtainable

Though there is no limit to the amount of goals you can set for yourself, putting a priority on your most desired goals will help ensure you remain focused on the accomplishments you want to complete the most.

The first step in the goal creation process is the brainstorming phase. Writing down all of your potential goals in one area allows you to compare and contrast each idea and identify which goals are the most important.

Once a goal has been selected and meets the four parameters for a suitable goal, the next step is to create a plan of action that identifies what specific task you are going to execute to achieve that goal.

Example One

Goal: Make ten bookings with a new travel supplier.

Parameters:

- Written Down
- Specific
- Measurable
- Realistic

Task:

- Take Supplier Offered Training
- Complete Certification and Specialist Exams
- Order Brochures, Sales, and Advisor Guides
- Connect with Sales Representatives and BDMs
- Experience Supplier's Product In-Person
- Promote and Market Supplier to Travelers

Example Two

Goal: Earn global travel professional certification.

Parameters:

- Written Down
- Specific
- Measurable
- Realistic

Task:

- Satisfy Pre-Requisite Requirements
- Study, Schedule, Take, and Pass Examination

Example Three

Goal: Increase annual bookings by $250,000.00.

Parameters:

- Written Down
- Specific
- Measurable
- Realistic

Task:

- Request Referrals from Current Clients
- Create an Online Group to Grow Client List
- Host In-Person Marketing Event with Supplier

Evaluating Performance

After your goals have been set for the year, keep your written list in a place where it can be viewed each day. This helps keep your desired results at the top of your mind throughout the year.

In addition to keeping your goals at the forefront of your daily thoughts, performing monthly evaluations can aid in achieving your goals in a variety of ways:

- Understand what is working. If the selected tasks for your goal are projecting you to meet or exceed your goal, you can keep everything as is or double down on these tasks to achieve way more than you thought was possible.

- Understand what isn't working. If the selected tasks for your goal are projecting you to come up short of your target, you can identify and implement new tasks to help get back on track.

- Provides motivation when you are able to appreciate what you accomplish each month.

Note that your written goals must be specific and measurable for you to be able to provide an accurate evaluation of your monthly performance.

Professional Development

Professional development is another part of the business and personal travel advisor growth process. Normally, a professional development task will align with your annual goals set each year.

The reality for travel advisors is that your experience and annual bookings grow over time. Though it is not impossible, it is very rare for advisors to make more than $2 million in bookings in their very first year. With so much industry training, networking, and marketing required to get yourself up to speed, it is only natural that it takes time to get yourself where you want to be.

Some advisors will experience linear growth, while others will experience exponential growth.

LINEAR GROWTH

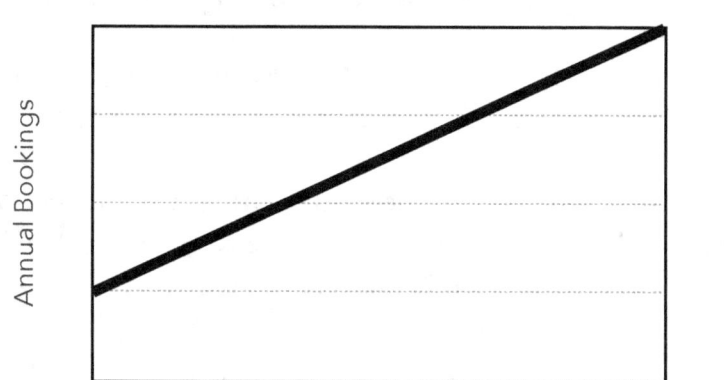

EXPONENTIAL GROWTH

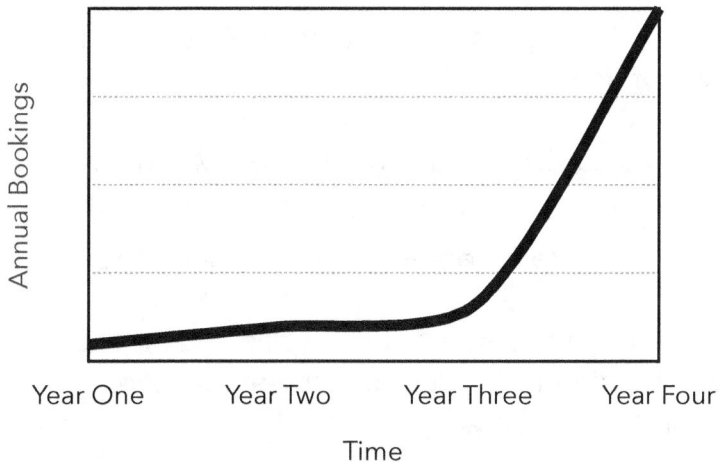

Generally, the more time spent in the professional development process, the quicker you can gain experience as a professional travel advisor. Typical professional development tasks include:

- Seminars & Conferences
- Initial & Recurrent Industry Training
- Property & Ship Inspections
- Personal & Supplier Experience Trips
- Credentials & Certifications
- Networking with Suppliers & Other Advisors
- Self-Education
- Mentorship
- Monitoring Trends & Utilizing New Practices
- Reviewing Industry Publications & Newsletters

Chapter Summary

Setting goals as a travel advisor can offer a variety of benefits:

- Clear Direction & Continuous Motivation
- Supply a List of Tasks, Actions, & Priorities
- Provide a Performance Measuring Tool

Written goals must be specific and measurable for you to be able to provide an accurate evaluation of your monthly performance.

9

Personally, I believe this final chapter of the book contains the most valuable information for travel advisors, as the material that follows describes all the different ways advisors can provide value to travelers.

Essentially, providing value to others is what drives people to utilize travel advisors, and if you can figure out how to continually provide value to others as a professional travel advisor, your earning potentials and personal fulfillment can be truly limitless.

The following compilation of ways you can help others as a professional advisor are all opportunities to meet the needs of an extremely wide range of people. Because a traveler's needs will vary from one person to the next, being able to fulfill more than one type of need can allow you to service a much larger range of travelers, thus creating substantially more demand for your business and services.

There are two main categories of needs that a travel advisor can fulfill:

1. Basic Needs
2. Travel-Specific Needs

Basic needs include all of the following:

- Safety & Security
- Food, Water, & Shelter
- Sleep
- Healthcare
- Connection
- Significance

Travel-specific needs include all of the following:

- Information
- Recommendations
- Assistance
- Professional Services
- Maximize Cost Effectiveness
- Eliminate Excess Expense

Generally speaking, there will be very little variation in what basic needs one traveler values over another, as most travelers would like all of their basic needs to be met.

Travel specific needs, on the other hand, will vary from traveler to traveler. For example, some travelers will contact you after they have their entire trip planned out and only need your assistance in obtaining the best price and amenities. However, other travelers may request you construct an entire expedition for them or provide recommendations from your personal experience.

Though you may be able to provide all six travel-specific needs to a traveler, finding out what each traveler values the most and focusing on that need is key. Once you can figure out the most valued travel-specific need for a client, the best thing you can do is find ways to provide the maximum value for that particular need.

Below are detailed ways to help meet each need and provide value as a professional travel advisor.

Basic Needs

Safety & Security

As a travel advisor, you can help keep clients safe and secure in the following ways:

- Ensure all travel suppliers selected for a trip have no history of safety or security concerns. If a client has already selected a supplier that presents a safety or security concern, make them aware of the potential threats.

- Utilize vetted vendors to provide private transportation where the transportation operator has their scheduled departure and arrival time on file with both their company, as well as the arrival or departure supplier. If possible, avoid transportation at night time.

- Avoid bookings that do not provide tracking throughout the journey.

- If a client is traveling alone or into a known high-crime area, provide on-site security or verified escorts during travel.

- Provide local law enforcement and embassy locations and contact information before departure.

- Notify the client of high-risk areas and what specific crimes take place in those areas so he or she knows what to be more aware of.

- Have the traveler make backup digital copies of all of his or her important documents. This is extremely helpful when a passport is lost or stolen, as most people do not know their passport number by heart.

- Provide GPS trackers that can be discreetly embedded in luggage and travel bags.

- Provide a list of products that can conceal personal valuables, while still being hidden on the body, instead of easy to steal locations, like a pocket.

- Make sure the client has adequate travel insurance or is able to sufficiently self-insure his or her belongings.

- If the client is a U.S. citizen, he or she has access to the STEP program. This allows the traveler to enroll his or her trip with the nearest U.S. embassy or consulate. The STEP program will help notify the traveler of a state of emergency, natural disaster occurrence, local civil unrest event, or family emergency.

- Advise the client to obtain both cell and data service during travel in case emergency communication or resources are needed, such as GPS navigation.

- Verify that the planned methods of payment by the client will be accepted at his or her intended destination, and also encourage clients to bring more than one method in case a backup method is required.

Food, Water, & Shelter

Food, water, and shelter normally are needs that are well taken care of while traveling, as travelers like to seek out the best places to stay, dine, and drink. Typically, when these three needs come under question of being fulfilled is when a reservation made in advance is not honored. This situation most commonly occurs when a supplier overbooks its available supply. In this scenario, the client needs these basic needs fulfilled by another supplier at the last second.

Additionally, when Mother Nature decides to alter travel plans for the masses all at once, travelers can find themselves scrambling and competing with other travelers when these limited resources are in a short supply.

The main difference between the two examples above is what type of options the supplier will provide when each occurs. Normally, if a supplier is unable to honor a reservation due to a fault of its own, such as overbooking, it will usually take on the responsibility and provide alternative options that will meet the need of the traveler.

If the supplier is unable to honor the reservation due to a force outside of its control, such as Mother Nature, then the client will need a new way to meet these needs without the assistance of a supplier. As a professional travel advisor, being able to help a traveler in these moments of need can be extremely valuable.

Usually, when events like these occur, a lot of changes need to be made in a very short amount of time. Stress levels are increased due to uncertainty of basic needs being met and can be compounded by disappointment in not reaching a planned destination, especially when traveling to relax and decompress.

The following are ways you can help meet the last minute food, water, and shelter needs for a traveler and help reduce the negative impact these additional tasks create:

- Locate and Secure New Accommodations
- Arrange Transportation
- Cancel or Modify Previous Reservations
- Compile Documentation for Insurance Claims
- Research Food and Beverage Options

Sleep

Though some travelers say they can run on low or no sleep, the reality of life is that the human body needs sleep. Without it, we cannot survive. Normally, the better quality of sleep a person can receive, the more energy they will have available for the following day.

Though it may seem like there is not much you can do as an advisor to better the quality of sleep for your traveler, there are a lot of factors you have control over to help create the best sleeping environment possible.

- Book high floor rooms, especially for stays inside a major city where street noise can exist 24 hours of the day.

- Verify accommodations have climate control, such as heating and air conditioning, especially in the summer.

- Request the specific bed, sheet, and pillow type preferred by the traveler.

- Avoid red-eye and overnight flights if possible. If mandatory, search for aircraft that offer lie-flat seats.

- Ensure flight itineraries that exceed 30 hours have a minimum 12 hour layover period with accommodations at an airport hotel for either day use or an overnight rest period.

- Provide links to jet lag applications to help adjust to local time more quickly.

Healthcare

Surprisingly, healthcare is sometimes one of the last things a traveler thinks about, especially for travelers with no pre-existing conditions. This means that many travelers are unaware of the nearest hospital location or the local emergency phone number while traveling. In an emergency, this can be critical information.

Recommendations for adequate travel insurance that covers medical expenses can also be made to help the traveler avoid financial loss.

Connection

Connection is normally one of the first needs travel advisors meet, as relationships begin at first contact. Though the type of relationship and the information you share with each traveler will be different, sharing any past experiences or life stories between each party will create an immediate sense of connection.

If you continually reach out to share life updates, as well as travel photos and videos from your personal trips, clients will (normally) feel a heightened level of connection with each interaction.

Significance

Filling the need of significance as a travel advisor can be accomplished in a variety of ways. As long as the traveler feels that they matter and are appreciated in some way by your actions, you have fulfilled this need.

Simple actions, such as mailing a hand written thank you note or having gifts waiting for them at their accommodations, can give them a sense of importance.

Travel-Specific Needs

Information

As travel professionals, travel advisors are well educated on a wide variety of industry policies and procedures. Additionally, advisors are well equipped with resources to locate accurate information so that we are able to give the most reliable information to travelers.

There are three main categories of resources you can provide to travelers to help increase their quality of life while traveling:

1. Time
2. Money
3. Energy

An example of information you could provide travelers that would save them time could be: expedited international customs processing options. Depending on the port of entry, there could be a registered travel program, such as the U.S. based Global Entry program. There can be dedicated fast-track lines for all passenger types, if they utilize online declaration forms such as the mobile passport program. There can even be paid priority options at some locations.

An example of information you could provide travelers that would save them money could be international phone and data plan options. With the implementation of e-SIMs in modern smartphones, travelers can use applications downloaded from the app store that may offer lower cell and data rates than their home country provider.

An example of information you could provide travelers that would save them energy could be luggage forwarding services. These services allow travelers to have their suitcases picked up at the home doorstep and transported to their destination accommodations before the traveler arrives.

Recommendations

Providing professional travel recommendations can help introduce travelers to a whole new world of experiences they never knew existed. In addition to being able to familiarize travelers to the thousands of different suppliers around the globe, you can provide excellent recommendations for common travel needs:

- Best Places to Dine
- Best Places to Stay
- How to Get Around
- Top Sights to See
- Popular Tours and Activities

One of the best tools available to advisors, that many travelers are unaware of, is the capability for advisors to recommend higher end rooms and suites that are not listed on public facing booking portals.

Normally, if a traveler searches for availability directly on a supplier website, he or she will be completely unaware of the hidden inventory rooms, unless a travel advisor brings it to his or her attention.

Assistance

Travel advisors are able to provide assistance to travelers before, during, and after their trips. When requested by the traveler, the professional travel advisor can help and advocate for the client when needed. As every traveler will vary, so will the type and level of assistance needed.

Professional Services

Though the particular services offered by a professional travel advisor can vary from one advisor to another, generally advisors will offer more than just basic booking services. The following are a few additional services advisors can offer that increase value to travelers:

- Escort Travelers in Person
- Passport and Visa Assistance
- Custom-Built Trips
- Points and Miles Consultations
- Arrange Special Requests With Suppliers

Maximize Cost-Effectiveness

Maximizing cost-effectiveness is essentially getting as much value as you can for a traveler at a particular price. The three biggest ways you can accomplish this as an advisor is through complimentary value adds, re-quote and re-reserve for a higher class of service, and booking travelers directly with suppliers.

As a refresher, complimentary value adds are additional perks and benefits advisors can include in standard booking rates, if associated with a consortium or supplier preferred agency program. The following are common value benefits:

Hotel and Resort:
- Amenity or Property Credit, Typically $100
- Welcome Gift or Amenity
- Complimentary Breakfast
- Upgrade (If Available)
- Early Check-In and Late Check-Out
- Complimentary Wi-Fi

Cruise:
- On-board Credits
- Prepaid Gratuities
- Bonus Amenities and Welcome Gifts

The next technique travel advisors can use to maximize cost-effectiveness for travelers is re-quoting and re-reserving refundable bookings for higher classes of service and accommodations. Normally, once a traveler has made a booking with a supplier, he or she typically leaves his or her reservation untouched. Doing so locks him or her into the booking price and accommodation type selected on the date of booking.

As time passes after the date of booking, if a supplier is trying to fill its open inventory, it can elect to lower prices to entice more bookings. If this occurs, advisors can select upgraded rooms and suites that are now the same price as the previous standard booking and cancel the previous refundable reservation. In this scenario, the traveler is now booked in a higher category at no additional cost to him or her.

Additionally, making bookings via direct booking methods, instead of third-party portals, helps increase the cost-effectiveness for a traveler. As a reminder, the following are common benefits of booking direct:

- Brand Status Recognition and Benefits (if a membership or loyalty program is offered)

- Membership Points and Miles Accruals for Future Complimentary Travel Redemptions (if a membership or loyalty program is offered)

- Guest Covered by Supplier Cancelation and Change Policies

- In-Person Customer Service

- Elevated Guest Experience (priority upgrades and amenities)

Note that almost all suppliers will price match a third-party booking. So if a client says he or she can find a cheaper price somewhere else, you can apply for a price match to achieve the same booking rate while enjoying the direct booking benefits.

Eliminate Excess Expense

Eliminating excess expenses for travelers is the process of lowering booking cost to the absolute lowest price. This provides the traveler with instant monetary value. The following are common ways to lower trip costs for travelers:

- Provide a Discounted Rate If Possible
- Apply All Eligible Promotions
- Verify Method of Payment Rebates
- Utilize Discounted Upgrades
- Re-Quote and Re-reserve

If able, provide a discounted rate to the traveler via a price match with a wholesaler, a consortium negotiated rate, supplier-offered discounted agency rate, or general rate qualifier, such as a group rate.

Ensure all current promotions offered by the supplier are utilized to lower both the main rate of the booking, as well as the cost of amenities and add-ons, such as meal plans. If the supplier also has a method of payment rebate available, which can either be a rebate through a credit card issuer or a discounted gift card, these discount methods can be used to lower the cost of the booking.

Some suppliers will also participate in discounted upgrade programs after an initial reservation is made. These buy-up offers can be used to upgrade categories or class of service at lower rates than if the higher category was purchased straight away.

Advisors can also re-quote and re-reserve refundable reservations in the same category to lower the overall cost of the booking, in lieu of selecting an upgraded room at the same cost.

Note that when fulfilling these needs, some resources will be available to advisors that are not available to clients. These could be items such as a dedicated agent support line or supplier sales team member who does not communicate with the general public.

Chapter Summary

Travel advisors have the ability to create immense value for travelers. Identifying what a traveler values the most and maximizing your impact for that need will keep your travelers coming back to you, trip after trip.

Basic Needs Include All of the Following:

- Safety & Security
- Food, Water, & Shelter
- Sleep
- Healthcare
- Connection
- Significance

Travel Specific Needs Include All of the Following:

- Information
- Recommendations
- Assistance
- Professional Services
- Maximize Cost Effectiveness
- Eliminate Excess Expense

Conclusion

Firstly, I would like to give a thank you to those who read this book in its entirety. I hope that the time you spent reading through the preceding content provided a wealth of knowledge and answers to your questions about the travel advisor profession.

Next, I would like to thank Brittany Morrison and her contribution to the foreword of this book. I met Brittany when she was entering the travel advising industry and noticed right from the start that she was going to operate on an entirely different level than most.

For travelers who are lucky enough to work with Brittany, I hope that her professionalism and value as an advisor are truly appreciated. The services she provides as a professional travel advisor are, without question, exceptional.

I would also like to thank the many advisors I have met over the years who inspired me to write this book. After listening to those eager to enter the field and realizing that each one of them was asking the same questions I was in the beginning, I knew I could figure out a way to help.

In my mind, becoming a travel advisor is a profession that so many well-traveled individuals can both enjoy and excel at. Not only are you providing value to others, which can help provide a great sense of purpose, the occupational characteristics and traits for most travel advisors are extremely sought after vocation qualities.

Though some advisors will be employed by a supplier, vendor, or corporate travel department, the majority of travel advisors who operate their own unique travel companies can enjoy the following working environments:

Remote Work

With booking capabilities available via phone, email, and online portals, advisors have the opportunity to work from home or anywhere in the world they desire.

No Boss or Coworkers

When working for yourself, you never have to worry about a boss or a coworker making your life difficult or stressful. Since there are no management or authoritative figures that control your professional future, you are able to do things the way you like them to be done.

Choose Who You Work With

Normally, employees are forced to work with each and every client who walks through the door of a business, no matter how pleasant or difficult they may be. Travel advisors, on the other hand, get to choose who they want to advise for. If a traveler you are making bookings for mistreats you or continuously causes issues with suppliers, you can simply tell them to find another advisor.

Set Your Own Hours

With no required clock-in or clock-out time or minimum amount of days working, travel advisors have the luxury of working when they prefer and how often they prefer.

Earning Potential

Since travel advisors do not earn a set salary and, instead, earn commissions from travel suppliers for making bookings, there is no cap to the amount of commission advisors can earn. Simply put, the more bookings you can make, the more you can earn each year.

Although travel advising offers so many positive qualities in regards to working conditions and sense of purpose from helping others, the industry is in desperate need of more well-traveled professionals who can provide value to travelers.

My wish is that this book finds its way into the hands of every individual who loves to travel and offers a lending hand to others. The better we can staff the industry with quality advisors, the larger the difference we can make on travelers' lives.

For those of you out there who understand this purpose and the value that this profession provides to both yourself and others, I wish you all the best as you enter the industry.

-*Taylor Beckett*

Additional Resources

Business Resources

- Small Business Administration
- Taxes for Travel Agents
- Trademark Engine
- GoDaddy
- Wix
- Dun & Bradstreet
- Better Business Bureau
- MyCompanyWorks
- Sunshine Corporate Filings
- California Registered Agent
- DocuSign
- Promotions Now
- VistaPrint
- PromoLeaf
- Smartpress

Travel Resources

- Agent at Home
- Flight Connections
- Aerolopa
- FrequentMiler
- TravelPulse
- Airalo
- Special Needs Group

Common Industry Acronyms & Abbreviations

AAA, American Automobile Association

The American Automobile Association, commonly referred to as "triple A," is a not-for-profit membership organization operated in the United States. This membership program provides discounts to a variety of travel suppliers.

ACC, Accredited Cruise Counsellor

The Accredited Cruise Counsellor certification (ACC) is a Cruise Lines International Association certification available to travel advisors who are accredited by CLIA and complete the certification requirements.

AI, All inclusive

All inclusive packages and rates are booking fares that include accommodation as well food and drinks.

ANR, Average Nightly Rate

Average nightly rate is a calculated rate identifying the average per night rate for a reservation. If a reservation had the following six nightly rates, the average nightly rate would be $270.83.

- Night one $200 (Check-In)
- Night two $200
- Night three $275
- Night four $350
- Night five $350
- Night six $250 (Check-Out)

APAC, Asia-Pacific

Asia Pacific is the geographic area located on the western side of the Pacific Ocean.

AP, Advance Purchase

Advanced purchase rates, also known as Prepay rates, are rates that require full payment at time of booking. These rates are almost always nonrefundable. Due to these two restrictions, suppliers will normally offer a 5-30% discount from the rack rate for clients who are okay with losing these two benefits.

ATW, Around The World

Around the world tickets are single airfare itineraries that allow a traveler to visit a wide range of global cities while making his or her way around the world in a particular direction.

B&B, Bed & Breakfast

Bed and breakfast accommodations are typically located at family owned guest houses and small boutique hotels. These lodging locations include both accommodation and a morning meal.

BAR, Best Available Rate

Best available rate is the lowest publicly available rate for a particular room on a particular night. This demand-based pricing model will cause fluctuations in price depending on expected occupancy levels.

BDM, Business Development Manager

Business development managers are supplier employees tasked with the job to help increase sales and drive business growth for the supplier.

BTA, Business Travel Account

A business travel account is a centralized payment account for businesses and their travel expenses.

BTB, Back To Back

Back to back sailings are consecutive sailings one right after the other. These type of bookings are most common for one way itineraries that start and end at different ports. When combined, the two one-way sailings turn the sailing into a round-trip itinerary that starts and finishes in the same port of call.

CAA, Canadian Automobile Association

The Canadian Automobile Association is a not-for-profit membership organization operated in Canada. This membership program provides discounts to a variety of travel suppliers.

CAT, Category

Accommodation categories exist in the cruise sector and are utilized to specify the category type of a room. For large ships, these categories can be listed by letter from A-Z, while smaller ships with only a handful of category types can use custom category identifiers, such as BS for Balcony Suite.

CB, Continental Breakfast

Continental breakfast is the designation used to identify a very light breakfast offering by a supplier. Continental breakfasts normally include select juices, coffee, bakery items, and fruit.

CCC, Certified Cruise Counsellor

The Certified Cruise Counsellor certification (CCC) is a Cruise Lines International Association certification available to travel advisors who are accredited by CLIA and complete the certification requirements.

CDW, Collision Damage Waiver

Collision damage waiver is an optional insurance product used to waive the traveler's responsibility in the event of a rental car accident, if operated under the rental terms and agreements. A collision damage waiver may or may not include coverage from theft.

CMP, Certified Meeting Planner

The Certified Meeting Planner certification (CMP) is a designation offered by the Meeting Professionals International (MPI) association.

CONUS, Continental United States

The Continental United States, also referred to as the mainland U.S., consists of the lower forty-eight states. This area of the U.S. does not include Hawaii, Alaska, or any of the U.S. territories.

CRM, Customer Relationship Management

Customer relationship management software offers a variety of tools to advisors. Though the offerings from each software provider can vary, the following tools are normally included:

- Create Itineraries and Trip Quotes
- Store Client Details
- Trip Calendars and Deadline Reminders
- Credit Card Authorization Forms
- Flight Monitoring
- Lead Management and Booking Logs

CS, Code Share

A code share is an agreement between two airlines where each airline is allowed to sell seats on the other carrier's flights. If an airline sells a seat on the other code share airline's flight, the airline not operating the flight physically can utilize its own unique flight number.

CTA, Certified Travel Associate

The Certified Travel Associate (CTA) certification is a certification course offered by The Travel Institute.

CTC, Certified Travel Counselor

The Certified Travel Counselor (CTC) certification is a certification course offered by The Travel Institute.

CTD, Corporate Travel Department

Corporate travel departments are in-house travel departments that book travel exclusively for company personnel.

CTIE, Certified Travel Industry Executive

The Certified Travel Industry Executive (CTIE) certification is a certification course offered by The Travel Institute.

CTP, Certified Tour Professional

The Certified Tour Professional (CTP) designation is a certification program offered by the National Tour Association.

CXLD, Cancelled

When a flight, hotel, or cruise reservation is canceled and the reservation software utilizes operating status codes, CXLD will appear on the status or live reservation page to designate a cancelled booking or flight.

DBC, Denied Boarding Compensation

Denied boarding compensation is the government required supplier payment that is mandated when a passenger is denied boarding due to a factor controlled by the airline.

DMC, Destination Management Company

Destination management companies are entities that connect local suppliers and travel service providers with travel advisors. DMCs are a great choice for packaged trips that include accommodations, tours, and transportation.

DMO, Destination Marketing Organization

Tourism destination marketing organizations are organizations that promote a particular location as an appealing travel or tourist destination. These types of organizations can be centered around entire countries or even a local town.

DOS, Director of Sales

The director of sales for a travel supplier is the head of the suppliers' sales team. Regional sales members who communicate frequently with travel advisors report to the director of sales.

E&O, Errors & Omission

Errors and Omissions Insurance, also referred to as E&O insurance or professional liability insurance, is a professional business insurance that normally covers the following items:

- Inaccurate Advice (You Tell Clients Their Hotel Has Free Parking by Mistake)

- Negligence (You Fail to Cancel a Reservation Before the Penalty Period Begins)

- Errors (You Booked the Wrong Check-Out Date)

- Omissions (You Forget to Tell the Client That His or Her Hotel Will Charge an Additional Resort Fee on Arrival)

ECC, Elite Cruise Counselor

The Elite Cruise Counsellor certification (ECC) is a Cruise Lines International Association certification available to travel advisors who are accredited by CLIA and complete the certification requirements.

ECON, Economy

Economy class is an airline specific class of service. Typical airline cabin classes include:

- Economy
- Premium Economy
- Domestic First
- International Business
- International First

ETA, Estimated Time of Arrival

Estimated time of arrival is commonly utilized in the aviation sector and refers to a flight's expected time of arrival. ETAs will normally fluctuate while in flight.

ETD, Estimated Time of Departure

Estimated time of departure is also commonly utilized in the aviation sector and refers to a flight's expected time off of the gate. ETDs will fluctuate with delays.

FAM, Familiarization Trip

Supplier familiarization trips are in-person educational experience trips. Suppliers offer these trips to advisors to increase their product knowledge and experience. In turn, this helps the advisor send more clients to those suppliers.

FB, Full-Board

Full-board is the designation for included meal plans provided by accommodations. These plans may or may not include drinks. Typically, it is more common to see full-board plans without drinks.

FC, First Class

First class is an airline specific class of service. Note that domestic first class in the United States is a completely different class of service compared to international carriers that offer first class on wide body aircraft. Domestic first class in the United States is considered a lower class than international business class.

FCC, Future Cruise Credit

A future cruise credit is a certificate or voucher that can be used towards future cruise fares and travel.

FFN, Frequent Flyer Number

Frequent flyer numbers are airline reward program numbers that can be utilized by passengers to earn miles on qualifying flights and outside activities.

FIT, Free and Independent Traveler

Free and independent travelers are individuals or small groups who plan their own trips and travel outside of pre-planned tour operators.

FOP, Form of Payment

Form of payment refers to the method of payment used to complete the purchase of travel goods and services. Most travel vendors will restrict accepted forms of payment to credit cards and cash.

GDS, Global Distribution System

The global distribution system is a worldwide reservation program that displays live travel supplier availability to authorized system users.

GST, Goods & Service Tax

Goods and services tax, also referred to as a value-added tax, is a government imposed tax on goods and services.

GTP, Global Travel Professional

The Global Travel Professional certification (GTP) is a Global Business Travel Association certification.

GTY, Guarantee

A guarantee cabin or stateroom is a reservation for an unassigned cabin aboard a cruise ship. This means that cruise passengers do not get to choose their particular cabin as it will be assigned by the cruise line.

HB, Half-Board

Half-board is the designation for meal plans provided by accommodations. Normally, half-board will include breakfast and dinner only. These plans may or may not include drinks. It is more common to see half-board plans without drinks.

ICA, Independent Contractor Advisor

Independent contractor advisors are professional travel advisors who utilize host agency credentials to capture commissionable bookings with suppliers.

IDL, International Date Line

The international date line is a time boundary line located in the Pacific Ocean that differentiates one day from another. This date line extends from the North Pole to the South Pole and dictates if a day is lost or gained, depending on the direction of travel.

LCC, Low Cost Carrier

Low cost carriers are budget fare airlines that specialize in selling basic airfare tickets. These types of tickets normally only include the seat on the aircraft, as well as a small personal item. Carry-on bags, checked bags, seat selection, snacks, drinks, and ticket change options are normally only available at an additional cost.

LCF, Local Currency Fare

Local currency fares are supplier fares for travel goods and services that are advertised and displayed in local currency. Some suppliers will offer currency conversion tools, while others will require the traveler to convert the fare to figure out the cost in his or her local currency.

LDW, Loss Damage Waiver

Loss damage waiver is an optional insurance product used to waive the travelers' responsibility in the event of a rental car accident, if operated under the rental terms and agreements. A loss damage waiver may or may not include coverage from theft.

LIP, Lead in Price

Lead in prices are heavily advertised lowest price available fares. These fares are generally not widely available and normally include the lowest class of accommodations offered by the supplier.

MCC, Master Cruise Counsellor

The Master Cruise Counsellor certification (MCC) is a Cruise Lines International Association certification available to travel advisors who are accredited by CLIA and complete the certification requirements.

NBA, Narrow Body Aircraft

Narrow body aircraft, also referred to as single aisle aircraft, are commercial airline aircraft that are smaller in comparison to wide body aircraft. These planes normally seat between 50 and 230 passengers per aircraft and have a maximum flight time of 10 hours or less.

Below is a list of common narrow body aircraft:

Airbus	Boeing
A220	B717
A319	B727
A320	B737
A321	B757

Bombardier	Embraer
CRJ200	E170
CRJ700	E175
CRJ900	E190
CRJ1000	E195

NCF, Non-Commissionable Fees

Non-commissionable fees are segments of a booking's total fare that do not qualify for commissions. Taxes, fees, and other non-supplier issued charges that are collected by the supplier, will normally be excluded from the commission calculation total.

NDC, New Distribution Capability

New distribution capability is an airline focused booking technology that allows airlines to publish and sell a wider variety of products to travel agencies, in comparison to what they are able to offer via the GDS booking technology.

NET, Net Rate

Net rates are the lowest standard rates available from a supplier that do not include commission. These rates are typically 10-30% below the standard rack rate and do not offer any compensation to the advisor.

NR, Nonrefundable

Nonrefundable bookings are inflexible bookings that suppliers utilize to heavily restrict changes and refundability for cancelations.

NSHW, No-Show

No-show designations for booking reservations represent a booking that was never cancelled, but the traveling party did not show up for said reservation.

OBC, On-Board Credit

On-board credit refers to a monetary allotment travelers can utilize while on board a sailing itinerary. Normally, on-board credits cannot be cashed out and will expire if not utilized by the end of the sailing.

OBT, Online Booking Tool

Online booking tools are business and corporate travel booking tools that allow a company to offer a travel booking portal to employees with set controls, parameters, and booking restrictions.

OTA, Online Travel Agency

Online travel agencies are travel vendors that offer bookable supplier goods and services to travelers.

OW, One-Way

One-way is a directional indication for air, cruise, rental car, transportation, and tours that do not start and end at the same location. Note that one-way does not guarantee non-stop.

PE, Premium Economy

Premium economy is an airline specific class of service. Note that premium economy is a completely different class of service than economy class seats that offer extra leg room or recline. Premium economy is normally only offered on wide body aircraft.

PIF, Paid in Full

Paid in full is a payment identifier for a reservation that has been paid in full prior to arrival.

PNR, Passenger Name Record

Passenger name records are airline specific numbers that contain a variety of passenger data associated with a ticketed itinerary.

PP, Per Person

Per person is a price designation identifier notifying booking parties that displayed prices are per person and not per room or cabin.

PPDO, Per Person Double Occupancy

Per person double occupancy is a price designation identifier notifying booking parties that prices displayed are per person with the condition that at least two persons are booked per room or cabin.

ROH, Run of House

Run of house is a room type booking indicator utilized by hotels. Normally, run of house rooms are basic or standard rooms that are set aside for group bookings. The actual room type will vary depending on availability at time of check-in.

RR, Rack Rate

Rack rates, also known as the Best Available Rate (BAR) or standard rate, is the advertised rate provided by the supplier without any discounts applied. This is normally the first rate to populate when making a search directly on a supplier's booking website.

These rates are normally offered on a refundable status, unless booked inside the supplier's cancelation or penalty period. Additionally, in the hotel, tour, and rental car sector, suppliers will typically not charge the selected form of payment until arrival.

RT, Round-Trip

Round-trip is a directional indication for air, cruise, rental car, transportation, and tours that start and end at the same location. Note that round-trip does not guarantee non-stop.

SAS, Seminar at Sea

Seminars at sea are events and groups that offer educational sessions while aboard a cruise ship on a scheduled itinerary. Seminars at sea can be set up by the cruise line for travel advisor events or they can be set up by travel advisors for affinity groups.

SOT, Seller of Travel

Seller of travel licenses are state-issued licenses that allow travel agencies and travel advisors to legally operate in the state the license is issued. Currently, the following four states issue a seller of travel license: California, Florida, Hawaii, and Washington.

SS, Single Supplement

Single supplements are surcharges for solo travelers when a supplier prices an accommodation requiring a minimum of two travelers. In some cases, single supplements can be waived, while most of the time there will be a minimum of 25% surcharge above the per person price when a booking is made by a single individual.

TA, Travel Advisor

Travel advisors are professional individuals who can choose to work for a travel supplier, travel vendor, travel agency (either as an employee or independent contractor), or can start their own agency. These individuals assist travelers with a variety of travel services.

TAE, Travel Agency Executive

The Travel Agency Executive certification (TAE) is a Cruise Lines International Association certification available to management level travel professionals who are accredited by CLIA and complete the certification requirements.

TC & TCC, Trip Credit or Tour Conductor Credit

Trip credits and tour conductor credits are either bonus commissions in the form of an averaged fare from bookings within a group, or are complimentary accommodations provided to the advisor that can be utilized to accompany the group.

TMC, Travel Management Company

Travel management companies are travel agencies that manage corporate travel programs.

TSA, Transportation Security Administration

The transportation security administration exists to help protect the United States transportation sectors.

UP, Upgrade

Upgrade designations identify when a reservation has been moved to a higher class of service or accommodation category. Upgrades are typically awarded in order of status, if a loyalty program exists. Suppliers without a loyalty program normally prioritize direct bookings over third-party bookings when awarding upgrades.

VAT, Value-Added Tax

Value-added tax, sometimes referred to as a sales tax, is a consumption-based tax on goods and services. Some countries will allow travelers to receive a value-added tax refund if certain conditions are met.

VTA, Verified Travel Advisor

The verified travel advisor designation is a certification program offered by the American Society of Travel Advisors.

WBA, Wide Body Aircraft

Wide body aircraft, also referred to as twin aisle aircraft, are commercial airline aircraft that are larger in comparison to narrow body aircraft. These planes normally seat between 150 and 500 passengers per aircraft and have a maximum flight time of 22 hours or less.

Below is a list of common wide body aircraft:

Airbus	Boeing
A330	B747
A340	B767
A350	B777
A380	B787

WL, Waitlist

Waitlists, commonly referred to as standby list, are space available listing programs for travelers who do not have a guaranteed seat or cabin from a supplier. Typically, travelers on the standby list will show up to the departure with the intent of filling a last minute no-show.

About the Author

Taylor is a professional travel advisor and owner of the Luxury Corporate Travel company, headquartered in the United States. In addition to being an author, he is the father to identical twin boys.

After graduating from Embry-Riddle Aeronautical University and becoming an airline pilot, Taylor founded his travel company (Luxury Corporate Travel). Each year, he sets out to visit at least two new countries and explore the world's most pristine destinations.

His mission is to operate the number one host agency for professional travel advisors and to help travelers get a better value out of their travel booking, which he believes makes a significant impact on people's lives. Normally, people will travel with those closest to them during their time away from work to rest, recover, explore, and decompress together. These periods of time are usually the most valued moments each year, thus the meaningful impact that can be made.

To learn more about Luxury Corporate Travel visit: luxurycorporatetravel.com